PERSPECTIVE
IS A VERB

PERSPECTIVE IS A VERB

101 REFLECTIONS ON GRATITUDE, AWARENESS, AND PURPOSE FOR A MEANINGFUL LIFE

THE CONVERSE COWBOY

HOUNDSTOOTH
PRESS

COPYRIGHT © 2025 MIKE ROBERTS
All rights reserved.

PERSPECTIVE IS A VERB
101 Reflections on Gratitude, Awareness, and Purpose for a Meaningful Life
First Edition

ISBN 978-1-5445-5004-6 *Hardcover*
      978-1-5445-5003-9 *Paperback*
      978-1-5445-5005-3 *Ebook*

INTRODUCTION

I once had a very close friend who seemed to have it all. He had worked his way up the corporate ladder and landed the gig of his dreams. Now he was earning a six-figure income and driving a company car. His personal life was also on point: he had married a pretty girl, and they built a big new house on three hundred acres with a fleet of new vehicles in the multicar garage. He had checked all the boxes that were supposed to equal success, yet all he could feel was self-doubt because he didn't have "more."

My friend in this story is a slow learner, so it took him years to understand that everything he was working for was an endless search for happiness on the hedonic treadmill. The route he was taking would bring temporary joy and excitement from time to time; however, he was trying to find happiness from other people and from material things outside of himself.

He had everything that one could dream of. In fact, he was living "the American dream"...yet he could not seem to quench the thirst from his soul. He knew and felt something was missing, yet he just couldn't figure it out. He couldn't navigate through the self-doubt and self-judgment. He was too concerned to open up to his friends about how he was feeling in fear of their criticism, and he worried that he might appear to be less perfect than he portrayed himself. His ego would never let that happen.

One day, after being gone for a few days on a business trip, he returns home. He barely has time to set his luggage down before his wife hits him with some news:

"I want a divorce..."

Unsure how to respond, he replies with "What do you mean?"

He knew exactly what those words meant, and he knew why she was saying them too. Their marriage had been rocky from the very beginning, but he couldn't admit that to himself; again, his ego wouldn't let him.

His life for the next few months was a bit of a roller coaster. All his self-doubt and worries were amplified. In his mind, he knew the imperfections of his "perfect life" were about to be exposed. Everything he had done to build his reputation was about to be tarnished once people started to find out that he was getting a divorce and that he wasn't perfect. He stumbled through life for the next few months, trying to avoid friends and family as much as he could. With tears in his eyes, he moved most of his belongings into a storage unit and rented a small apartment in town.

He lived there for six months, with only the basic living essentials. White walls, bright white lights; being there felt like living in a hospital. The dream had become a nightmare. He would wake up, barely be able to drag himself out of bed, go to work, come home, eat a TV dinner, and go to sleep as soon as his sleeping pills kicked in, which was the only way he could settle his mind enough to doze off every night. He was a wreck.

This may sound like the end of the road, but it is actually where his journey of self-discovery begins.

He could barely get out of bed some days, his mind filled with depressive thoughts. He was miserable, and he finally realized that it was all self-induced. He began reading as many books as he could about human psychology and different philosophies about life. He slowly began to find some of the answers to the questions he didn't even know that he had.

Getting out of bed in the mornings became easier. His perspective was beginning to shift. He realized that he was human, he had flaws, but he was not *flawed*. He started to be a little kinder to himself. He began to accept himself. This was a pivotal moment in his life, and over the next couple of years, he experienced tremendous personal growth and learned more about his human experience. He became Grateful for his ex-wife having the courage to make the decision to separate and for how that decision ultimately changed his life for the better.

My friend in this story is doing well today and is still on his journey of self-discovery.

Every time I see him in the mirror, I remind him to Stay Grateful!

. . .

This book started as a stack of journals from that tumultuous and transformative time. That rough patch sent me down the road of looking for answers, and I found them in dozens of books, which I read to recalibrate. I found centuries of wisdom and perspective from philosophers, seekers, and survivors who became mentors I will never meet. I developed a simple practice of writing down quotes that resonated with me from those books and journaled what those words meant to me.

By reflecting on these philosophies, I cultivate them in my life. My hope in letting you read my journal is that these notes will help you do the same. Maybe you'll write down your own notes from this book or from one you discover in these pages. This is a book I hope you reread, gift to others, regift, and keep coming back to again and again. My hope is that you won't simply reflect on these pages but use them as prompts to prime your perspective and develop the habits that set you up for a life of Gratitude, Awareness, and Purpose.

Perspective is a verb. As humans, we have the opportunity to choose our perspective. You never know what's good or bad in the moment. Life is happening *for* you and not *to* you. When faced with circumstances you can't change, you are forced to change your perspective, and that can change everything. Everything happening in your life is the absolute best thing that can happen for you at that time.

We must be intentional; otherwise, we will default to the negative hardwiring our brains have been conditioned to for survival. The human mind is constantly being conditioned and has been throughout our entire lives, since the moment we were born. The content we consume, the thoughts we think, and the words we say and hear play a role in our conditioning. Much like priming a pump, we can intentionally prime our brains for the thoughts and experiences we want to have.

Why is this important? I feel like most people aren't even aware of this. They may think they are in control, but they are merely going through the motions of life, blindly putting one foot in front of the other. As I describe throughout the book, awareness is the first step. If you don't have the awareness to know that you can choose your perspective, it will be chosen for you.

I've found that I must consistently expand my awareness. How can we make a change if we aren't aware it's necessary? Both expanding our awareness and overcoming resistance require stillness of mind. By consistently taking the time to slow down, breathe, and recognize our own thought process, we'll broaden our awareness, which will allow us to recognize the opportunities to be Grateful for and confidently make the necessary changes. It's time to make a change.

By finding stillness through Gratitude, our mind and body align and get in tune, becoming more aware; we're better able to mentally override our unconscious habits. Gratitude is the closest thing we have to a superpower and, broadly speaking, something we can never have too much of.

Over the years, as those stacks of journals piled higher and the lessons from them manifested in my life, my practice expanded to include sharing these quotes and reflections on social media. I started @theconversecowboy on Instagram, and one day I shared a photo of myself in my everyday attire—a cowboy hat, pearl snap shirt, jeans, and Converse sneakers—holding up a poster quote. When something takes off and finds an audience on social media, it's easy to get lost in the metrics, and if you're not careful, you can get confused about why you started sharing in the first place. But if you keep your eye on your original intention, sharing becomes a practice every bit as profound as time spent alone with the private pages of your journal. Putting your words out there teaches you to be okay with people not always aligning with what you have to say. Haters are out there, but more often than not, the act of sharing brings about connection. When you make your struggles known, you learn how universal so many of life's problems can be. What I learned from being vulnerable was that I wasn't the only one going through a rough patch. I wasn't the only one left deeply unfulfilled by consumerism and "checking boxes."

I've learned that when I get the Awareness and Gratitude parts right, the Purpose naturally reveals itself to me. My mind isn't distracted by nonsense. I am very tuned into what is most important to me at any given moment. Awareness and Gratitude require effort and inner work. Putting in the work in these two areas allows your purpose to flow to you and enables you to authentically flow through your work.

Now it's your turn. Use this book as a blueprint for self-discovery. Lean into the discomfort of a new writing habit or push yourself to go further than you've ever gone before. Use the poster quotes at the top of each page as your own prompt and see where your mind goes. There is zero room for self-judgment throughout your growth process. Self-judgment is just another form of ignorance—a lack of awareness. Everyone you look up to today didn't start where you see them today. Seek to understand what it takes to become your best self, wherever you are and with what you have. But the most important thing is to start that journey today, right now. Keep rolling down the runway of life and take off. Once you do, you'll fly to a perspective and understanding that you've never known before. Enjoy the ride.

Stay Grateful!

NOTE TO THE READER

Many of the quotes in this book are attributed to "Unknown." This is to say that my research either came up with no known origin or disputed origins. The internet actually makes the work of verifying quotes even harder because wrongly attributed quotes are posted and reposted everywhere alongside accurate ones. Certain figures like Albert Einstein and Marilyn Monroe are misquoted so often that any quote attributed to them is suspect. Other quotes are more like parables or ancient wisdom that have been repeated many times in many different phrasings, making their original form impossible to source. For example, "Good decisions come from experience...Experience comes from making bad decisions" has been attributed to Mark Twain, among others, but its true origin is unknown. Wherever I encountered murky or unknown origins, I listed the attribution as

"Unknown." The last thing I want to do is put more misquoting or lazy requoting out in the world. As Ben Franklin once said, "You can't believe everything you read on the internet."

Wherever the poster quote is not in quotation marks, the origin is me, a.k.a. The Converse Cowboy.

IF I COULD ONLY HAVE ONE MANTRA TO LIVE BY every day, this would be it.

Gratitude is the closest thing we have to a superpower—one that any of us can access at any time. Gratitude is always only one choice away.

A small pivot can shift your perspective, and a shift in your daily perspective can change your entire life. Gratitude is a way of setting yourself up for those transformative moments. When you prime your perspective with Gratitude, you will quiet that inner voice within, and your fears and doubts will be replaced with a more optimistic viewpoint. You will start to see more clearly, and you'll begin to recognize opportunities when they present themselves.

Proactively implementing Gratitude sets you up for better days than if you were to start with a bunch of expectations—a list of demands. A simple smile of Gratitude the moment you wake up sets the tone for your day and is a nod to the universe, saying, "Thank you" for another opportunity to experience this beautiful life.

Expectations aren't inherently bad. They are necessary. I'm a firm believer that what gets measured gets managed. But this isn't an either/or proposition. It is possible to root our expectations in Gratitude. We can have desires, set high expectations, but understanding why certain things happen the way they do is determined by our interpretation. Expectations not playing out as we envision could be the best thing that happens *for* us. We can have expectations without being controlled by them. Proactively implementing Gratitude throughout our lives provides a healthy meaning and purpose for any situation or circumstance we may encounter.

Would the world be a better or worse place if more people implemented more Gratitude? We all know the answer. Why then do we choose to ignore this superpower that every conscious being has access to?

Expectations rooted in Gratitude are essential for sustainable personal growth. Gratitude offers the ultimate freedom we all seek—the freedom to choose to have a really good day.

No MATTER WHERE YOU ARE IN LIFE OR WHAT you're pursuing, I'll let you in on a little secret: most people you look up to are winging it. They simply started from where they were with what they had, and opportunities were presented to them along their journey, simply from showing up consistently with a focused intent.

We tend to wait to get started instead of just starting. Everything will not be perfect, and you won't know everything you need to know. There are tools and resources you do not yet have that will make whatever you're doing more efficient and more effective.

No matter how broken or flawed you think you are, the world needs your color, your style, your personality, and your craft. Keep showing up and follow the process, not the prize.

OFTEN, WE GET SO CAUGHT IN THE TRAP OF chasing our dreams and goals that we forget to recognize the many gifts all around us. As ambitious people, we constantly seek to improve and search for the proverbial "more."

Gratitude isn't about diminishing your dreams and goals. Never feel guilty for wanting more or wanting something better. But the key to achieving more than you could ever dream possible is to start with Gratitude for what you already have. Without the practice of Gratitude for what you already have now, you won't appreciate "more" when you get it. You will continue on the hedonic treadmill of constantly chasing the next shiny object you think will make you *happy*. Most people will never wake up to this. They will remain unaware as they continue to stack one pursuit after another, only to experience a fleeting joy that disappears almost as fast as it showed up.

The good news is waking up is simple. But there is work to be done. Slow down and take a moment to reflect, recognizing what you have to be Grateful for in this moment. This could be something as simple as a warm cup of coffee in your hand or the clear blue sky outside your window, or even having a window (not everyone does). If you can't think of anything and you're feeling hopeless, but you wish you didn't... believe it or not, you can be Grateful for that discomfort that makes you want to change.

Every action you take is a nod to the type of person you wish to become. No single instance will transform your beliefs, but as they build up, so does the evidence of your new identity. This does not mean shutting the door on your past but instead understanding that every experience you've been through has shaped the person you are today. Even the hard stuff. *Especially* the hard stuff. The greatest souls are awakened out of suffering, and the most impressive personalities have endured many scars.

A LONG TIME AGO IN WEST TEXAS, A POOR FARmer lost his horse. All his neighbors came to his house and said, "We heard the news of your horse running off. That's too bad."

"We'll see..." said the farmer.

The next day, the horse came back and brought a herd of wild horses with it.

"Well, that's great," said the neighbors.

"We'll see..." said the farmer.

The next day, the farmer's son was thrown from one of the wild horses while trying to tame it and broke his leg.

"That's too bad," said the neighbors.

"We'll see..." said the farmer.

The following day, the king's conscription officers came around to recruit young men for military service. They didn't take the boy because of his broken leg.

"Good news!" said the neighbors.

"We'll..." said the farmer.

Tap into the belief that everything happening in your life is the absolute best thing that can happen *for* you at that time, whether you initially think it is good or bad. We can't truly call something "good" or "bad" because we have no idea what each situation may lead to.

Many things that happen in life are out of our control. So the question is, why not choose to be Grateful for everything happening as if it's the best possible thing that could happen for you? We can accept it or we can fight it. The circumstances still exist.

The Stoics called this *Amor Fati*, love of fate. They knew we can make the best of everything that happens when we don't just accept but *love* what happens. It may sound odd to *love* an experience that feels like a tragedy or bad luck, but that attitude makes sense when you admit that you don't know where that experience might lead you or what you might learn from it.

We always have a choice. We have the freedom to choose our attitude and mindset in any situation. #ChooseGratitude

Look for the good, and opportunities will present themselves. They're much easier to see when you're looking for them. Often, the things we don't get will lead us to a more satisfied and fulfilled life.

OBSTACLES ARE OFTEN OPPORTUNITIES IN DISguise. We can never know what something may lead to. We must focus on what we can control. Remember the Serenity Prayer, and accept the things we cannot control, have the courage to change the things we can, and seek the wisdom to know the difference.

The many blessings and opportunities that are just below the surface of defeat and despair will not be readily apparent to us, especially as we're experiencing them. Struggle is a part of any journey worth being on. The secret is to focus on each step, one after another. Once you get a few small wins under your belt, you will begin to confidently welcome new challenges. You will have an understanding that discomfort is necessary for every next level of the person you are to become. Viewed through the most optimal perspective, every challenge or obstacle that comes our way is a gift.

So when you find yourself having a pity party, wishing things were different, asking, "Why me? Why this? Why now?"—trust that your situation could have a silver lining you haven't seen yet. (It almost always does.)

KEEP YOUR "WINDSHIELD" CLEAN AND HIGHLY visible. What is in front of us is more important than what's behind us. Allow yourself the freedom to dream big.

Clean your windshield by clearing your mind. Uncover the thoughts and narratives that are holding you back. Look back when necessary, learn from your past, reflect on what you might have done differently, but don't stare into the rearview. That's how accidents happen.

The future is uncertain and unknown, which can be scary, or it can be exciting. You get to choose your perspective; that is freedom. Distractions and noise are only noticed when we can see clearly. It is possible to slow our minds down while moving forward. Slowing down is sometimes the best way to speed up. Remember, some of your best days are yet to come.

WE HAVE BEEN CONDITIONED TO THINK THAT *more* is the answer. Unconsciously, we check the boxes of life we think will lead us to "happiness." I've been down that road and constantly have to expand my awareness so I don't end up there again.

Awareness is the first step toward Gratitude. You must first become aware of being Grateful, and the more Grateful you become, the more aware you will be; it's the law of being present.

To be truly Grateful is to be present. Pay attention to the things you have now and to what you have already achieved. Have Gratitude for them and for the people who helped you along the way.

Focus through the lens of Gratitude on even the smallest thing that assisted you along your journey. This act alone will set you up for future successes, almost more so than the act of what you did. Gratitude sets the scene and primes your perspective for opportunities to consistently flow your way.

When you implement the practice of Gratitude for what you already have, you are automatically in a state of abundance. You see clearly that you have *enough* and you are *enough*. The universe recognizes when you act from a state of abundance and when you operate from a state of lack. The difference is not in what you have; rather, it's in how you choose to think about what you have. Stay Grateful for what you already have, and the universe will work with you to continue to provide more for you to be Grateful for.

THE HUMAN MIND IS MUCH MORE POWERFUL than we can even comprehend.

Whichever belief you choose, you are right. You will find the evidence to support your belief. You will tune your awareness to seek things that back up what you think. We achieve what we believe we are capable of. This can be dangerous because it holds true for negative beliefs and self-doubt every bit as much as it does for positivity and Gratitude.

Slow your mind down. I'm sure we've all heard this at some point in our lives. What does it mean? The thoughts don't stop, and many of them come from the influence of others and society's expectations. In other words, they're not even your own thoughts. This becomes important because many of our ideas and beliefs around ambition, goals, hard work, success, and so on are products of that conditioning. That phenomenon can work for or against us.

To use self-belief to our advantage, there is a four-letter word we have to stay away from...

Can't is a word that comes all too easily to us. When trying something new, it's often the default answer. *Can't* is a fake friend. It feels like it's protecting us from falling flat on our faces, but what it really does is prevent us from trying in the first place.

Starting anything new or pursuing grandiose ideas and dreams requires a willingness to take risks. That is one characteristic of the professional mindset, an attitude that separates the dilettantes and dabblers from those who are truly committed.

Pros still have self-doubt; however, *can't* is not in their vocabulary. Pros ask, "How can I _____?"

HAVE YOU EVER NOTICED THE STREAM OF THOUGHTS that flood in as soon as you open your eyes in the morning? Where did those thoughts come from? I'm not here to say I have the answer to that mystery; however, I know we can have a significant influence on the thoughts we have. We can set the tone for the day, starting the night before.

Stop scrolling social media before you go to sleep. It's pointless, unhealthy, and you're not going to miss anything. Substitute mindless activity with a mindfulness practice.

One way to condition your mind is by becoming present in that moment and reflecting on the things you are Grateful for. Reflect by scanning from moment to moment throughout your day; you can take as long as you want, but you only need thirty seconds to a minute. Notice when your awareness slips, and recognize when you are more in tune. Feel the Gratitude deep within you. Think about the goals you want to achieve, and have Gratitude for them as if they are already yours. This act alone will set you up to be more present the next day from the moment you open your eyes. Done consistently, this is a practice that builds and compounds over time, feeding you with wisdom about your best self. (Rinse and repeat every day.)

Writing in a Gratitude journal before bed primes our subconscious (which will be running all night while we sleep) and unlocks the doors of opportunity to be revealed to us. By shifting our focus to the gifts that are all around us, we use our power of choice to move away from worry and lack to a state of Gratitude for what we already have. By becoming present, we expand our awareness, slow our thoughts down, and train our minds to become more still. If we can get this one practice right and implement it consistently, then our perspective for the day will shift, and we will experience a different "reality:" one that we intentionally cultivated.

By changing how we go to bed, we change the way we wake up, and transform our tomorrows. The smallest changes done consistently over time equal big results.

STUDIES SHOW THAT BY PROACTIVELY FEELING Gratitude within and expressing it toward others, we can override our negative thoughts before they come up.

When you express Gratitude for what you already have, the universe smiles at you and gives you more to be Grateful for. You're in tune and looking for the good; therefore, you notice more good. It's a mutual respect between you and the universe, one that is a virtuous cycle.

You become aware of opportunities that have been there all along; you just couldn't see them through the fog of negative thoughts, ingratitude, and self-doubt.

Gratitude isn't just about saying "thank you" when things are good—it's about recognizing the good even when things aren't perfect. When you focus on what you have instead of what you lack, life seems to open more doors. You attract better opportunities, build stronger relationships, and see possibilities where others see problems. It's not some mystical magic—it's just how perspective shapes reality. A Grateful heart doesn't mean life gets easier, but it does make the "hard" times more meaningful.

FOR MANY, THE JOURNEY TOWARD PURPOSE AND self-actualization starts with breaking bad habits and getting space from difficult people and situations.

Boundaries are the structure that lets you and those around you know what is most important to you. At first, some people in your life may be confused or give you pushback. Stand firm. Sooner or later, they'll learn how you expect to be treated, and they'll come to respect it, or they'll move on. Either way, you win.

You get to choose the boundaries you implement in your life.

If you allow yourself to settle for less, that is what will continue. If you allow yourself to be influenced by others, that too will continue.

If you choose to become conscious and aware of your thoughts and intentional with your actions, that will not only continue but evolve into a deeper understanding of yourself and the world as you know it. Your personality and perspective begin to shift in a way that alters *reality* in favor of your highest self.

ONE OF THE KINDEST THINGS WE CAN DO FOR ourselves is to focus our energy intently on Gratitude.

Gratitude is the key element for a healthy self-esteem, and a good self-esteem builds upon the feelings of Gratitude. They go hand in hand; however, the cycle must always begin with Gratitude.

Think of getting heat from an old-school fireplace. No one has ever walked up to their fireplace on a cold winter day and expected it to supply them with heat without first adding firewood and igniting a fire. Only then will heat come from your fireplace. And the more firewood you add, the more the fire builds, producing even more heat. Without first starting a fire, you'll just sit there cold and complaining and staring at your fireplace, wondering why it won't give you heat.

This is a very simple analogy yet a great comparison to Gratitude and self-esteem. Why do we look at ourselves with judgment and compare ourselves to others without first putting any wood on our fire? It is naive to think we can maintain a healthy self-esteem without first implementing Gratitude. And similar to adding more firewood to produce more heat, the more Gratitude we have, the higher our self-esteem becomes, and the higher our self-esteem, the more reason we have to be Grateful.

That's not to say ungrateful people can't have high self-esteem. They absolutely can! However, it is very fleeting and often comes across as delusional self-confidence, not the healthiest way to maintain true self-esteem that is sustainable.

Let's say you do something well. You receive praise for your efforts from those around you, and for a moment, you feel proud. Fast forward a couple of hours, and all those people singing your praises are gone. That proud feeling may linger for a little while longer, until the temporary joy runs out. Then what? There is no structure and no foundation to support your self-esteem.

The healthiest and most consistent way to maintain and build your self-esteem is with a solid foundation, one that is cultivated with Gratitude. Pro tip: it comes from within; you don't need anything or anyone to implement Gratitude.

The benefits of this recalibration of perspective start with your own well-being. You must know that Gratitude is contagious. Before long, the true benefits of your self-care will show up in the way you treat others and the way you make them feel about themselves.

WE MISTAKENLY OVERESTIMATE THE AMOUNT of attention that other people are focusing on us. This is called "the spotlight effect." The reality is they're too busy thinking about themselves. So why not do those "embarrassing" things you've been afraid to do or chase that ambitious goal instead of being stifled by fear of other people's judgments and opinions? Do what you want to do! There is freedom in being *okay* with what others may think or say about you.

We seldom stop to ask ourselves, *Why do I even care what they think?*

The most common question I hear from guests I have on *The Converse Cowboy Podcast*, once the cameras and mics are cut off, is "Was that okay?" It's so interesting to me that some of the most accomplished people still seek approval and are concerned about what other people think about them. Constantly seeking the approval of others can be crippling.

The morbid truth is everyone you see right now will be dead in one hundred years, so why pay any attention to what they're saying? Live your life on your terms and have the courage of a lion to walk your own path. Be willing to walk alone and not lose sleep over the opinions of people who are *not* doing better than you. This is not meant to be a judgment on those individuals; however, you are not obligated to entertain their opinions in any way.

When you walk into a room full of strangers and your ego flares up, thinking the spotlight is on you, and the self-doubt and negative thoughts start to creep in, try this. Use those thoughts as a trigger to shift your focus onto Gratitude. Focus your attention on wishing blessings to every person in the room. You'll first notice a smile inside, and it can't help but be expressed on your face. The negative thoughts fade quickly. Over time, this becomes a habit, and your internal narrative will begin to align with your best self. Rinse and repeat.

This is Gratitude; slight shifts in focus done consistently over time and with repetition become your personality.

IN MY OPINION, THIS IS ONE OF THE MOST IMPORTant philosophies in this book. If you can fully understand the meaning of this, then you'll be equipped to handle anything that comes your way. *Anything.*

Viktor Frankl, psychologist and bestselling author of *Man's Search for Meaning*, knew a thing or two about suffering. He was a Holocaust survivor. He witnessed his father die from starvation, and his mother and brother were both executed in the gas chamber along with many of his friends.

In *Man's Search for Meaning*, he tells of the horrors of his experience from being in four different concentration camps over a three-year period. When faced with so many tragedies, others gave up, but Frankl discovered a way to find meaning in the suffering he endured. He writes:

> Man *can* preserve a vestige of spiritual freedom, of independence of mind, even in such terrible conditions of psychic and physical stress.
>
> And there were always choices to make. Every day, every hour, offered the opportunity to make a decision, a decision which determined whether you would or would not submit to those powers which threatened to rob you of your very self, your inner freedom...Fundamentally, therefore, any man can, even under such circumstances, decide what shall become of him, mentally and spiritually.

After the war, Frankl devoted his work and writing to a form of psychology known as "logotherapy." Part therapy, part philosophy, this method addressed mental health and well-being at the level of purpose and meaning in life. His experience of the worst horrors imaginable helped him show others going through personal struggles, big and small, that they too had that power of choice.

Like most of Frankl's patients, most of us will never go through anything like what he experienced, but we all have that freedom: to choose our own attitude in any given situation.

IGNORANCE DOESN'T MEAN STUPIDITY; IT MEANS not knowing what you don't know. If you constantly go through the same struggles over and over, it might be time to hit pause and reflect. Recognize your patterns. Usually, it's a pattern of thoughts, actions, and reactions that creates your struggle.

This reminds me of a painter who did some work for me a few years ago. Every day, I'd show up to check on the jobsite, and it was the same miserable story from him every time. *I can't pay my bills...There's not enough work out there...I don't have the right equipment...* He was a great worker and still is; he just has a "Chicken Little" perspective. It got to the point that I would avoid him as much as possible. That sounds terrible, I know, but I chose not to be around his ignorance and negativity.

What are you choosing? Are you the person people avoid? Are you consciously choosing what you focus your attention and energy on, or are you merely going through life completely unaware you have a choice? You, and only you, are in control of your thoughts. Good thoughts must be cultivated.

> "There will come a time when you believe everything is finished. That will be the beginning."
>
> Louis L'Amour

WITH THE RIGHT PERSPECTIVE, WE CAN THRIVE along our journey. Every day is a new page, every year a new chapter. I often think about my life five years ago. It looked much different from what it does today. I am still *me*; however, my perspective is different, and my goals and ambitions have shifted.

Many millionaires have been bankrupt at least once. Many high achievers and highly successful people we see today have had to overcome struggles and challenges along their journey. They didn't give up or quit. They began again, this time with more knowledge and experience. The decisive factor was a willingness to take a positive, growth-based attitude toward failure, seeing it as a necessary step along the journey and not the end of something. Stacking knowledge from the lessons learned allows the compound effect to work in our favor.

No matter what you've attempted and failed, or maybe didn't go the way you wanted, know that it wasn't wasted time. You gained valuable insights that could only be learned through doing and through taking action. The most valuable source of knowledge is experience.

Stepping stones rarely resemble the final destination.

THE TRUTH IS EVERYONE IS STRUGGLING WITH something on some level. No amount of money or fame can exclude anyone from this fact. You'll never hear negative criticism from someone who is doing better than you, and if you do, then they just revealed to you that they are *not* doing better than you.

Observe but don't judge. Observing is simply viewing something or someone with an open mind. Pay close attention, without imposing your opinions, and seek to understand. Judgment is a close-minded, preconceived perspective that hinders further understanding.

We often judge and criticize before we seek to understand. You may not agree with someone's views or perspective about a particular topic, and that is fine. You are entitled to your opinion. However, until you fully understand someone else's point of view, there is no room for criticism.

Ask questions. Ask *great* questions. This alone is a great practice and will further your knowledge and give you insights into other people's perspectives. I truly believe the world would be a better place with more open-mindedness.

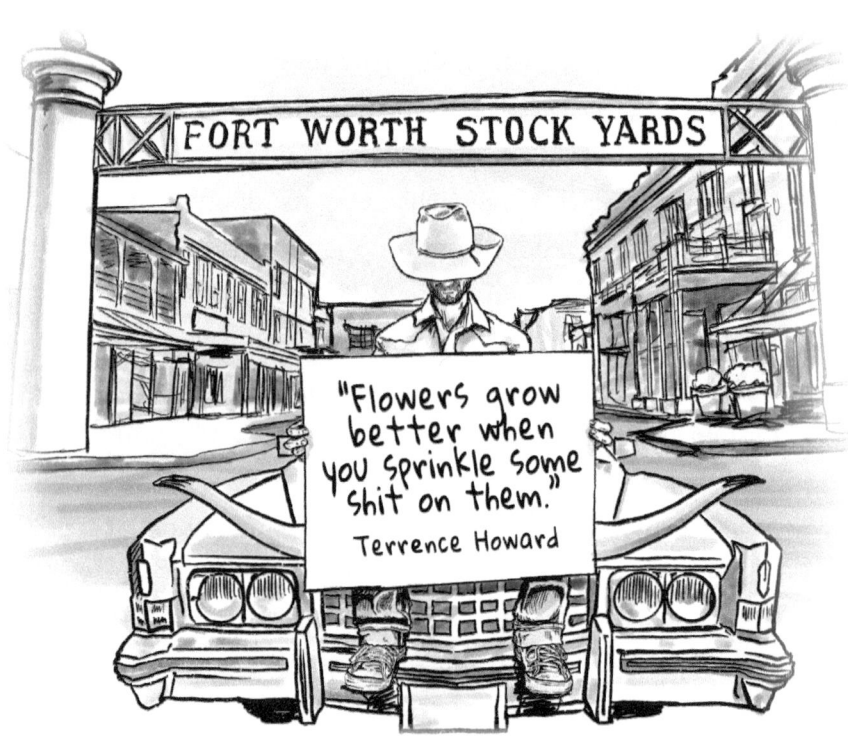

INTENTIONS ARE THE SEEDS WE PLANT. WITHOUT intentions, weeds will spread and infect your mind, making it hard to navigate any pursuit with clarity.

Along your journey, you will have plenty of *shit* that will help these seeds grow.

Growth requires some level of pain, not *suffering*. Choose the perspective to see the shit as a good thing, as an opportunity, and as necessary for you to realize your highest potential. The challenges you face today can be viewed in one of two ways: they can completely shut you down and leave you feeling overwhelmed, or they can be viewed as fertilizer that is needed to stimulate your growth. Get comfortable with being uncomfortable.

YOUR PAST DOES NOT PREDICT YOUR FUTURE. However, the lessons learned from our past can influence the person we become.

What you choose to do today *will* create your future. Our past can tell us a lot about the person we are today, and until we recognize what is influencing how we think and act, we'll stay on that same unconscious treadmill, going nowhere fast. We can learn from our past, but our past does not define who we are today or who we are to become in the future. Who we are right now, in this moment, is of ultimate importance.

Get curious, and seek to understand your behaviors. Of course, this might be frightening in the beginning, but the empowerment and freedom you gain from this practice will further your understanding of yourself.

Limiting beliefs only hold us back if we *believe* them. Don't be shackled by your own beliefs. After all, they're *your* beliefs, yours to change at any time.

THE BEHAVIORS AND HABITS YOU PERFORM EVERY day shape and reinforce the stories you have about yourself.

Conscious decisions train our subconscious how we want it to think and act. By focusing our attention and energy on the inner work required to become aware and to maintain Gratitude, we are essentially installing the hardware that will serve our highest self for years to come. Training your mind with your mind is a fascinating concept and one that can seem challenging at first, but over time, and with consistent repetition, our subconscious can carry the load that once took intense focus.

Much like a horse and rider. A horse's mind is wired for survival. They are flight animals. Anytime they sense or perceive danger, they'll flee to avoid it, even at the expense of self-preservation. Somewhat of a paradox, I know. The rider is the conscious mind, and the horse represents the subconscious. All great horsemen have a system for starting young colts. Though their techniques may differ, the one thing they have in common is working with and manipulating the horse's mind so it trusts the rider. They slowly build confidence in the young horse by introducing new things. Usually, this takes place in a small round pen. It's a very controlled environment, so if the horse decides to flee, no problem. It won't get too far, allowing the rider to effectively teach the young horse trust and a willingness to work together. The beginning can be very slow and delicate. Each horse is different and will progress on their own time. The horse cannot speak with words, but a trained rider can understand what the horse is saying through horsemanship. A horse's body language is how they communicate in the herd. Are their ears pinned? Are they looking at you? Is one ear on you and the other pointed in the other direction? Horses react to pressure and the release of pressure.

At some point, usually within the first couple of days of working with a young horse, the rider will introduce a saddle to the horse, working their way onto the horse's back and riding it for the first time. The horse almost every time will offer to buck as it runs around the round pen. Again, it can't go very far, but it wants one thing: it wants the rider and that bundle of leather called a saddle off its back, so it's going to do everything in its power to make that happen; run, buck, kick. What happens next is something that is fascinating to me every time I see it happen. At some point, the horse realizes the person sitting on their back and that bundle of leather isn't going anywhere, and they realize it really isn't causing them any harm. So they begin to go along in harmony with the rider.

I consider the elements of horsemanship to be very similar to those of training our minds. The point is that the conscious and the subconscious are similar in that we must give conscious attention and effort to train our subconscious. And know that the things we are focused on during that first ride will be on autopilot after thirty to sixty days of consistent riding. Consistency is key when working with horses, and so it is too when working with our minds. Going slowly in the beginning allows us to go faster later on.

Honest reflection is key and will not lead you astray. Your spirit will know if you are still on course or if you need to recalibrate your efforts.

THE STORIES WE HAVE REPEATED TO OURSELVES daily for years becomes our *reality*. Your thoughts are ***your*** *thoughts*. You have the freedom and the opportunity to keep thinking the same thoughts if they serve you well, or you get to shift them at any time. **Your perspective is your choice**.

Take a look at who you are today and where you are today. Your thoughts about yourself are what led you to this place. If you like what you see, keep going. If not, know that change is just one thought away.

WE TEND TO PROCRASTINATE AND DELAY LIVing our dreams mostly because of fear. Fear stems from self-doubt or fear of other people's opinions. Without awareness, our ego holds us back, in fear of failing or fear of the discomfort that "leveling up" requires.

Ego is that loud voice in your head, swearing it's the true you—your unconscious thoughts, unaware emotions, your job, your status. It's a trap, convincing you you're separate, always comparing or chasing validation. It clings to yesterday's regrets or tomorrow's worries, robbing you of your peace in the now. It's just a shadow, not your essence. Mindfulness cuts through—notice that voice is important, but don't buy into the ego's story. Step back, breathe, and anchor your mind in the present. Feel the moment, raw and unfiltered, where you're connected to something deeper, beyond the noise. That's freedom: living fully in this breath, this heartbeat, with Gratitude for what is.

The magic formula is to have Gratitude for who you are and where you are in this moment, while at the same time being Grateful for the opportunity to become an even better version of yourself. Often, it's hard to see our own incremental growth or just how far we've come. It's easier to see others' progress from a distance and easy to get caught up in the comparison game. We never know the opportunities that lie within our next effort. Success could literally be one thought or one action away. The very next call you make could change the trajectory of your life.

The seed of every habit is a single, tiny decision. And a decision that is repeated leads to a stronger habit. The roots of your habits begin to grow deep and wide, serving as an anchor for what is most important to you. This is also why bad habits are so hard to break; you are essentially uprooting an oak tree that has been growing for years or even decades. Remember that change can take years…until it happens all at once.

Before any change takes place, we must seek to understand where we're starting from. Once you fully embrace the person you are today, the evolution of your best self becomes a much clearer and more meaningful path. Change becomes possible when you become Grateful for where you are right now.

One of the kindest things we can do for ourselves is to focus our energy intently on Gratitude: remaining Grateful for every situation, for every person, for every relationship, and for every event that helped to mold you into the person you are today.

Once you accept *yourself* for who you are, the change you seek isn't coming from a place of judgment or disapproval. Rather, the change you seek stems from a more positive place; you are now seeking your highest future potential from your highest present potential.

Awareness is key to maintaining a perspective that allows you to continue to level up. Awareness allows you to recognize when you are giving your best effort and also when you may not be maximizing your potential. Realize that we all have good days and not-so-good days. There should be zero judgment, simply awareness and honest accountability. Recalibrate your mindset and your efforts as needed. This is called *personal growth*.

D*ELAYED GRATIFICATION* IS A SKILL FOUND IN almost every successful person...at least those who have sustained success over time. But I think that is only part of the equation. I believe they found gratification in the process rather than the result. The most successful people I know, and the ones whose work I admire most, get gratification from doing the work for its own sake.

It's not that they don't enjoy the material rewards; it's that those who are the most successful and the most fulfilled are more concerned with improving their craft through doing the work.

The key is to show up consistently for the work itself. Play the game for the love of the game, with Gratitude in focus for each and every opportunity that comes our way. When you focus on the process, even if you don't get the outcome you were hoping for, you still win because you come away transformed by the process.

YOU MAY THINK YOU'RE AVOIDING RISK BY "PLAYing it safe." But the truth is, nothing we do is without risk. When you choose to "play it safe," you risk living a life that feels bland and inauthentic. You risk giving up on your dreams. You risk being unhappy with your life and your choices.

For those times when we feel like we're failing, there is so much more going on behind the scenes of the universe that we don't even realize. When we say yes to ourselves and do what we truly love to do, we cultivate habits that make us better at our chosen craft.

Life experiences will stack in our favor when we intentionally pursue our dreams. We initiate the law of attraction, and, much like a magnet, we draw to us the things and people that support our dream. Just because you can't see it happening doesn't mean it isn't real. We can't see gravity either, but we all know if you drop an apple out of a tree, it will fall.

Believe in yourself and chase down your dreams. You will succeed or you will learn. You can't lose.

INTENTIONAL GOAL SETTING IS, WITHOUT A DOUBT, a very productive practice. With our compass set, we strike out to achieve our goals as fast as we possibly can. Once achieved, we set our goals even higher, recalibrate the compass for our new heading, and go at it again.

In recent years, I've learned to leave room for spontaneity. Often, the most memorable moments that happen along our journey are never planned. They show up when we allow ourselves and our curiosity to explore, leading us down a path that even our most conscious self never could've imagined.

As ambitious people, we set very high goals and live with strict discipline to achieve those goals, which is why we are successful...but where's the flavor? After a while, the experience of living becomes more valuable than any goal achieved. The experiences of lessons learned and the people you unexpectedly meet along the way are essential to living a fulfilled life.

Most everyone has felt lost at some point in their life. Nobody has everything 100 percent figured out. If they say they do, they're lying to themselves and to you. And if they truly believe they do, they are simply placing limits on themselves. Our conscious mind can only comprehend a fraction of our true potential.

Embarking on the journey from the person you are today to the person you wish to become, you are sure to get lost along the way, and that is okay. That feeling of being lost should let you know you're on the right track to truly experiencing life.

Being lost in the right direction is something we should try more often, or at least be more accepting of it when it happens. The frustrations and the impatience we feel from not seeing results fast enough are a natural side effect of ambition. Use these feelings as a trigger to get more curious about yourself and seek to understand your mind on a deeper level. When we allow ourselves to become lost in a moment or in a situation that wasn't planned, that is when the magic happens. If we knew and believed that everything that happened in our lives was the absolute best thing for us at that moment, would we allow ourselves the freedom to enjoy each situation? Opportunities present themselves in ways you could not have imagined.

Surrendering to the process may seem counterintuitive and might be challenging for most ambitious people; however, letting go is a skill, and like most skills, it becomes better with consistent practice.

The question to ask yourself is not where will you end up but what experiences you want to have along the way.

EXTERNAL THINGS ARE NEVER THE PROBLEM. It's our assessment of them we must pay attention to. Where does complaining get you? If something doesn't go your way or you're uncomfortable, do you improve the situation by whining? Wouldn't that energy be better spent on taking action or accepting the problem and moving on? If you accept the obstacle and work with a clear intention, an alternative solution will present itself. You can then create your life experience one thought and one action at a time.

This is the power of *positive thinking*. Because it's an overused term and often misunderstood, let me lay it out for you. Positive thinking does not mean living in a fantasy land and ignoring the difficulties life may present. It means embracing them as opportunities for growth. Positive thinking simply opens the door to endless possibilities.

Complaining is a denial of those possibilities. It's a way of digging in your heels, staying stuck, and making it all about you. Positivity is an acknowledgment that this, too, shall pass.

Remember, we have the ability to choose our own attitude in any given situation. Everything in life is happening *for* you...look for the good.

SITTING ON THE COUCH, EATING POPCORN, AND watching Netflix is comfortable and relaxing. However, once that is over, what do you do next? Scroll social media? Check email? Search for the next dopamine hit?

It's easy in this day and age to be comfortable. Almost everything you need is within reach, and every distraction imaginable is just a click away. But that also means it's easier than ever to stay stuck.

The Converse Cowboy followers and podcast listeners reach out with questions every week. By far, the number one question I get asked is "How do I find my purpose?" You are the only one qualified to answer that question, but I can give you a hint...you're most likely not going to find it in a *comfort zone*.

The truth about "finding your purpose" is you find it on the other side of challenges, obstacles, and focused intention. Getting outside of our comfort zones is where we'll meet our best selves. What was once uncomfortable becomes comfortable, and we must rinse and repeat, finding the next uncomfortable situation that will elevate our potential once again.

We must build the layers of our character over time. Your best today is different from what it will be in just five years. We often get overwhelmed by trying to do too much in a short amount of time when the proven blueprint is to gradually build over time.

THE MOST PRACTICAL WAY TO CHANGE WHO YOU are is to change what you do. James Clear's *Atomic Habits* is a great book on why this is true and how to harness the power of habit to your advantage.

Habits are unique and often overlooked as a tool to help us get where we want to go in life. Instead of thinking about personal growth in terms of an abstract ideal of the person you want to become, think about what that future self would *do*.

Is that person a morning person? Try getting in the habit of going to bed earlier.

Is that person well-read? Make time to read every day.

Is that person outgoing and upbeat? Smile at the people you encounter throughout your day.

You'll be astonished at how the benefits of these habits compound in your life and who you become as a result of these changes.

As Clear points out, **small changes over time equal big results**.

THE PROGRESS WE'RE MAKING IS OFTEN SLOW to reveal itself.

Think about a seed buried deep within the earth. From the outside, it may seem like nothing is happening, but beneath the surface, a miracle unfolds. Roots establish themselves, breaking through the soil, and a shoot emerges, reaching for the sky. Likewise, our hard work acts as the roots that establish a strong foundation, while the doors that await us represent the blossoming shoot, just waiting to be discovered.

Steve Jobs, co-founder of Apple, once said, "You can't connect the dots looking forward; you can only connect them looking backward." This profound insight highlights the inherent uncertainty as we embark on our personal quests. We may not know exactly where our hard work will lead us or how it will manifest in the future. We must cultivate the mindset that everything we encounter along our journey is the absolute best possible thing that can happen *for* us at that time.

Every moment spent improving our craft, expanding our knowledge, and pushing our boundaries sets in motion a series of events that will eventually reveal those hidden opportunities.

This introspection acts as a compass, guiding you toward the doors that align with your passions and purpose. It is through self-reflection and awareness that we gain the clarity needed to recognize the doors that were there all along, waiting patiently for us to discover and open them.

WHEN YOU FIND YOURSELF AMONG PEOPLE who live their lives in a way that doesn't align with your values, you can choose to be Grateful for your awareness to recognize this and do something about it.

People will surprise us. Actions speak louder than words. Someone may reveal to you that they aren't the person you once thought they were. Maybe you found out about some things they said or did behind your back. These are things that are out of your control, and there should be zero regret for being a good person to them. The same goes for marriages that don't work out or anyone who has caused emotional harm to you. Seek to understand their motivations; have the awareness that whatever has happened is a reflection of the other person, not of you.

Do not be phased by these negative interactions. How we judge ourselves is how we judge others. Focus on being kinder to yourself, and in turn, you will be more kind to others. You have nothing to feel bad about if that kindness isn't reciprocated or received the way you thought it would be.

Being a good person means being honest and always doing what is right. You can never be wrong by doing the right thing in kind. Maintaining Gratitude and practicing kindness is vital for making the world a better place to live.

Such a powerful question. When would you ever say, "Nah, I don't want to recognize the opportunities that are all around me. I'd rather stay in a state of misery and dwell in my negative thoughts."

In a state of awareness and fully present, you would never consciously choose to not be Grateful. The only reason we lose sight of this is because we are ignorant and lack awareness.

Gratitude stimulates our awareness, and the more aware we become, the more Gratitude we will find throughout our lives. The more Grateful and aware we are, the more present we become. It's a beautiful cycle that begins with Gratitude. Implement Gratitude in your life so you can have the awareness to recognize when others may be in need of your light. You'll be amazed at the positive impact this attitude has on others as well as yourself.

THE AMATEUR LIVES IN FEAR OF MAKING MIStakes and is paralyzed by that fear. The pro uses mistakes, learns from them, and moves forward.

Meaning and purpose are found through experiencing experiences. We gain insights through doing. Good decisions come from intelligent interpretations of what we are experiencing.

Stay Grateful for each and every one of your experiences because they are the building blocks that cultivated the person you are today.

The only thing worse than making a wrong decision is not making a decision. When you stay frozen by resistance, you miss out on the lessons you could learn by trying something (anything!) and coming away with lessons learned from having it not go to plan.

Sometimes, ready, shoot, aim is the best approach. Make a decision! Learn from experience. Rinse, repeat.

BOTH *SUFFERING* AND *GRATITUDE* ARE A CHOICE. Most likely, the choice of "suffering" comes by default, through unconscious thinking, whereas Gratitude is most often a more conscious choice that requires intentional effort.

We can choose to use the pain for motivation rather than fall victim to *suffering*.

When we direct our attention and energy toward Gratitude, we align with the present moment. And the more present we become, the more aware we are, making it much easier to feel Grateful. It's a cyclical process. Being present, awareness, and Gratitude all feed off of one another.

Gratitude is an acknowledgment of the good that is in your life. The *good* may very well be disguised. You are the one pulling the *levers* that provide the meaning. Remember, you have the freedom to choose your focus.

The negative thoughts that seem to pop into our minds by default will linger and have lingered for years, unnoticed but very much affecting our day-to-day lives. The thoughts that serve the betterment of our well-being are earned through awareness and the recognition that we direct our own thoughts.

Realizing that we can choose Gratitude at any time and in any given situation is empowering.

Gratitude is the most undervalued and underappreciated virtue we have as humans today.

Do not be deceived into thinking your actions are of no consequence. Every deed, no matter how small, weaves itself into the greater order of things. Just as the hand is part of the body, so too are you part of the whole—what you do affects the fabric of existence.

If you act with wisdom, justice, and temperance, you strengthen not only yourself but all around you. If you neglect duty, indulge in idleness, or believe your efforts are meaningless, you diminish not only your own soul but the world itself.

The work of today may not reveal its fruits immediately, yet nature teaches us that nothing grows without time. So act not for immediate reward but because it is right. To live with purpose is its own reward, and to uphold virtue is to shape the world, even in ways unseen.

The act of showing up to do the work and committing to your purpose is bound to have positive results way beyond your intended outcome. Seeing you show up every day might inspire strangers or even your friends to go after their own dreams. Your loved ones will benefit from being around the happiest version of yourself when you're living for your purpose. The work you do behind the scenes will have an impact when your work is presented to the world.

Live as though your deeds matter—because they do.

THE OPPORTUNITY TO HAVE A POSITIVE IMPACT on someone else's life is available to each and every one of us every single day. And yes, it could be as simple as a smile.

A smile has the most impact when face to face, but a genuine smile can be felt over a phone call or through a text or email. A smile signals to others and yourself a certain kindness within. A smile settles the mind and alludes to a warm sense that everything is okay.

Sometimes a smile can be as good as a hug or an authentic embrace.

Be the first to smile at a stranger on the street. There's something very powerful about setting the tone for an interaction, even if it's merely passing a stranger and neither of you ever speaks a word. That is an opportunity to present a smile to someone's life who may desperately need it.

Smiles are contagious and reciprocal, thanks to our brain's mirror neurons. When we see someone smile, we are likely to smile back, creating a ripple effect of positivity. Think about any time you've been in the presence of a baby smiling or laughing. It is warming and contagious, continuing to be passed on and on from one person to the next. A smile from someone else initiates a natural and often involuntary reaction within us.

Scientific studies have found that smiling actually makes us happier, causing neurons to fire in parts of the brain that correspond with contentment and a sense of well-being and boost our immune system as well. Sports physiologists have even found that smiling and seeing others smile can have a positive influence on sports performance and endurance.

The pencil experiment is a simple yet fascinating psychological study on how physical actions can influence emotions. Participants are asked to hold a pencil in their mouth in two different ways. First, they grip the pencil with their teeth, which naturally forces their facial muscles into a smile-like position. They hold this for a few seconds while rating their mood. Next, they hold the pencil with their lips, pushing their mouth into a frown-like shape, and again rate their mood. The idea, rooted in the facial feedback hypothesis, is that the act of smiling—even if forced—can make you feel happier, while frowning can dampen your mood. In the "smile" condition, the pencil activates the zygomaticus major muscle, mimicking a genuine smile, often leading to a slight mood boost. In the "frown" condition, the opposite happens, as the muscles mimic sadness. This experiment, often credited to studies like Strack et al. (1988), demonstrates how our body's actions can subtly influence our emotions, offering a playful way to explore the mind-body connection.

It may very well be the person staring back at you in the mirror who needs to feel your kindness today. A smile is an easy way to recalibrate your perspective.

OUR PERSPECTIVE BECOMES OUR REALITY. There is only one like it. Sure, there may be similar views and understanding, but *your reality* is yours only. You are the creator and director of your own story.

Our perspective is shaped by Gratitude, which is the key that opens the doors of opportunity, revealing to us a clearer and more accurate vision. Know that opportunities rarely have "opportunity" in the subject line. They often come disguised as misfortune or temporary defeats. Through the lens of Gratitude, we are able to find the good and interpret the meaning of any situation. It is easier to find the good when we are looking for it.

It's like looking "everywhere" for your sunglasses only to find them on your head. There are opportunities all around us. We are often distracted by our own agendas or what others may think. Our minds are conditioned by society and by our environment. Opportunities are often hidden by the distractions we see outside, yet we've had them all along, just like your sunglasses.

It is our duty to seek it out.

PEOPLE WHO AREN'T ON YOUR LEVEL ARE GOING to criticize. Words can be painful only if we allow them to be. We have the ability to choose how we react. The words of others have no meaning except for the meaning we give to them. We can choose to be Grateful for these people and for their words because they have given us the opportunity to overcome yet another obstacle, further building our character and confidence within ourselves. We can choose to use criticisms as fuel that gives us energy instead of allowing them to stifle the realization of our dreams.

I WONDER HOW MANY THINGS NEVER CAME TO fruition for humanity due to the doubt in someone's mind. How many songs remain unwritten, or which inventions were never created because someone lacked the courage to say yes to themselves?

Self-doubt is crippling. It is also the unconscious response to failure and the fear of failure. The best way to fight the battle against doubt is with awareness, along with genuine curiosity, clear intentions, and honest effort.

We can't fight that which we don't know exists. So, we must first become aware of the doubts we have—and rest assured, we all have them. Bring them out of the shadows and into the light. Then get curious. Seek to understand where your doubts come from. After all, they were created in your mind. The same mind that created your doubts has the power to extinguish them.

Focus your attention on what you want to manifest. Set your intention and show up with consistent effort, then surrender the outcome to a higher power. Always remember, you're entitled to the effort, not the outcome.

With consistent and intentional effort, your doubts and inhibitions will slowly fade away and be replaced with powerful thoughts that serve your best self.

WORRY IS BASED ON FEAR. BESTSELLING AUTHOR Robert Kiyosaki refers to fear as:

False
Evidence
Appearing
Real.

We do not react to what happens; rather, we react to our perception of what happens. We take that false narrative and run with it, and we burn a lot of energy in the process.

The opposite of fear and worry is to focus on the present. Focus on what you can control and accept, and let go of the things that are out of your control. The key is to take action on the things you can control.

I'M NOT NAIVE THAT WE HAVE CERTAIN LIMITAtions. I also know that most humans rarely realize their full potential. This happens because of the limits we put on ourselves, without ever knowing that is what we are doing. We get caught up in our stories and are influenced by society. Every one of us is guilty of unconsciously putting limits on ourselves, myself included.

Most limitations exist solely in our minds. We created these limiting beliefs and attached them to our identity. In the process, we reinforce our beliefs about what is "realistic" and "unrealistic." I am constantly seeking what most people would deem as "unrealistic" goals.

For me, to live any other way would just be boring.

We must become aware of our thoughts that play on a loop and seek to understand if they are enhancing or limiting our well-being. We are capable of achieving far more than we can even comprehend.

WE HAVE BEEN CONDITIONED TO THINK THAT *more* is a goal unto itself. Especially here in the United States.

We place value on things that are difficult to attain, and then once we get them, we are often left unfulfilled and our desires unsatiated; we immediately begin a new search for *more*, thinking this will be the cure for the fulfillment and satisfaction we long for.

Fully understanding our values is the first step in the pursuit of "happiness." Why do we want what we want? What will it do for our overall well-being if we attain our desires?

Once I get (blank), then I can be happy is a lie, and the sooner we realize this, the sooner we can begin our journey to true happiness. We must recognize our attachments and let them go with the understanding that happiness only comes from within.

WE ONLY SEE THE *MASK* THAT PEOPLE PRESent to us. Even those people who are close to us hide behind a mask. We only see the version others want to present to the world. No matter how well we think we may know our friends and family, we truly have zero clue about what is going through someone's mind on a daily basis.

I reflect on the people I knew who have committed suicide. The same questions get asked each time. *What? How? Why? They seemed so happy. I had no idea.*

Suicide remains one of the leading causes of death throughout the world, and its rates are often higher in societies with more resources and material wealth. According to the Centers for Disease Control and Prevention (CDC) WISQARS Leading Causes of Death Reports, in 2022: there are nearly twice as many suicides in the United States every year as there are homicides.

Everyone you encounter has something they are struggling with. Some challenges are more severe than others, but we're all still struggling, nonetheless. Know that behind the mask that is presented to the world is a vulnerable human being seeking to find purpose and importance in our world. We never know what others are going through mentally. Unlike viewing external injuries, such as a cast on a broken arm or leg, we often can't accurately see someone's mental well-being.

If you are someone struggling, I encourage you to seek help. You've survived every one of your bad days so far,

and with professional guidance, you can navigate your way through whatever it is you're going through.

If you're looking for a sign not to kill yourself, this is it! Don't let suicide be a permanent solution to a temporary problem. It is not a weakness to ask for help.

Remember to be patient with others. You have zero clue as to what they may be going through mentally. Understand that we must see things and people as they are, not as you are. Allow yourself to be seen, and in turn, you will see others.

We can sit in a room and think about doing something all day long. We can have the best plan drawn out, but until we take action, that is all it will be. Of course, starting with a great plan is a key element to success, but there comes a time when we must implement said plan. That is when the lessons are learned and when the opportunities begin to show up.

You don't know what you don't know. Once you begin your journey, you'll be amazed at how many doors of opportunity open for you. You'll gain wisdom along the way, and your character and your personality will be shaped and molded by your thoughts and by your actions.

Keep showing up consistently every day with a focused intent and in a state of Gratitude, and your path will reveal itself to you.

THE MAGIC HAPPENS WHEN WE SHOW UP CONsistently every day. The universe recognizes our efforts and our intentions. Like a snowball rolling down a hill, it gets bigger and gains momentum. If something stops it, the start will be slow. An object at rest wants to stay at rest, and an object in motion wants to stay in motion. This is Newton's First Law of Motion, also known as the Law of Inertia. Inertia is an object's resistance to changes in its state of motion.

I equate this to pursuing your dreams. In the beginning, it's easier for some because we don't have any expectations that slow us down or, worse yet, stop us from our pursuit. We simply show up and do the work. That is the purest form of showing up to improve our craft. It's okay to slow down or even pivot, but we must not stop or, worse yet, never begin.

Writer's block, procrastination. All too often, we form a story as to why we can't do a certain thing, and we never begin. Enter the muse. The muse knows when we show up to do our work. Ask any legit songwriter how they can write such profound lyrics, and they'll tell you it comes from something outside of them. But they did their part and showed up. Seek to understand your resistance. What is it you fear? Why are you not showing up for yourself and others?

I like the journal prompt of writing a letter to your eighty-five-year-old self that has already achieved everything you've ever wanted. I do this monthly. You'll be amazed at the insights that flow to you. Some things you thought were important will actually be revealed to be irrelevant, and other things you are procrastinating on will be understood as necessary.

There is no hack for showing up and doing the work. Every person you see that you admire has spent many hours, days, years, and sometimes decades honing their craft. They make it seem effortless. Anytime you see this, respect their dedication to the process.

The magic happens when you combine intentional thought with consistent action.

THIS QUOTE IS A BRUTALLY HONEST REMINDER to truly *live* every day, not just merely exist.

Every day we're on this earth, we're simultaneously living and dying. Which option do you choose to experience? As far as I know, we have a finite time, and we each have an unknown expiration date. Every day that goes by is owned by death. I've recently been asking myself: *Am I living more than I'm dying today? Am I living with intent or aimlessly going about my days?*

You are the person you are today because of the things you did yesterday. You will become the person you are tomorrow because of the things you do today. Consciously or unconsciously, the compound effect of your daily actions is impacting your life.

Be Grateful for the person you are today, and at the same time, be Grateful for the opportunity to become a better version of yourself every day.

SELF-CONSCIOUSNESS AND ANXIETY ARE A TRAP. All that we see in front of us is how we feel inside our heads.

Anxiety and excitement are like cousins. They are both feelings that stem from thought. We think about a game we have coming up, a performance, a speech, or maybe a test. We get excited and/or we get anxious. We feel both of these emotions as we think about the *unknown* in wonderment. Where the two split from excitement to anxiety is when our thoughts lean more to the side of worry. We then get nervous about the outcome, the negative self-talk begins, and it's usually a downward spiral from there.

The solution is awareness. We can feel the anxiety and observe it without listening to it.

We have conditioned ourselves to feel this way, and it has become our normal. Anxiety will most likely never lead you to the results you desire. Become aware of your thoughts. Recognize them for what they are, gently and respectfully dismiss them from your mind, and redirect your focus onto what excites you.

Our energy flows to where our attention goes.

Isn't that interesting? Our mind is our greatest asset and extremely powerful, and at the same time, it can be our biggest liability. Much like a loaded gun, it can be used for good or for bad, depending who's finger is on the trigger.

Our self-talk, our daily narrative, has a greater impact on our daily lives than I think we realize. We have on average between 60k to 70k thoughts every single day, according to research by Dr. Joe Dispenza. Thoughts aren't inherently good or bad, but how we choose to think about them is what determines the outcome and how we feel about it.

Picture logs floating down a river. If you're trying to jump onto every one of them, you will find yourself in burnout pretty quickly. It is entirely possible to stand on the shore and watch the logs—your thoughts—float by, observing each one without judgment. And every now and then, you may consciously choose to hop on a particular log and ride it down the river a bit. All the while noticing the other logs that steadily float past.

Become aware of the thoughts that are holding you back from your best self. Know that you have a choice, and you decide what you will believe. The stories we tell ourselves about ourselves become our reality.

Remember you are the creator and the director of your reality.

OUR "FEARS" ARE OFTEN CREATED IN OUR OWN minds. We place limits on ourselves through our self-talk. Fears are normal and shouldn't be judged but, rather, observed with curiosity: questioning where our fears come from and why they are there, bringing them out of the dark and into the light.

Just about every fear we humans encounter can be traced back to evolution. Fear of not fitting into a tribe meant death. Fear of eating the wrong berries meant death. Fear of a lion hiding behind a tree meant death. We are hardwired with adaptive fears at birth for survival. Those fears that kept our ancestors alive no longer serve us today, yet they are part of the software we're born with. They were developed over time and must be reprogrammed over time. Fear, as it relates to personal growth and being the best version of you, often shows up in the form of "ego"—that inner voice that says, "Don't try that, you'll look stupid," or "don't do that, you're not ready yet."

Allow curiosity to lead the way; seek to understand more about your fears.

What if you overcame your fears and achieved the "impossible?" What if you were **bold** and altered your self-talk? What could you achieve? Think about every human who has ever achieved greatness. At some point, they consciously overcame their fears.

Practice being curious, and over time, you will quiet the negative chatter in your mind, revealing your true potential to yourself.

"It is a fault to wish to be understood before we have made ourselves clear to ourselves."
Simone Weil

BEFORE YOU WORRY ABOUT BEING MISUNDERstood, be sure you know who you are.

Every successful business has a mission statement. They know what they're about and they know how they operate. We each have our own mission statement in life. Some of us are intentional and know exactly what is important to us, and others rely on others to tell them what is important.

Do yourself a favor and write your own mission statement. What are your values? What do you want to experience? Who do you want to surround yourself with? Why do you do what you do? When you understand who you are, you won't have to wish to be understood anymore because you will embody what you value. You will come to know and understand your purpose.

This is a process that never ends. A continued opportunity to seek understanding for who you are each day.

THE RESISTANCE WE FEEL TO DOING THE THINGS we are called to do often stems from a fear of what others may say or think. Sitting on the sidelines, not doing anything because of what we think others might criticize, is a guaranteed way to avoid criticism. It's also a recipe for doing nothing with your life.

Every human is original. We each have DNA that has never existed before, and we each have unique talents to offer to the world. Think about all the courageous people who have made this place better to live in through their art or inventions or ideas. How different would life be if they had never taken action on their ideas because they thought others might criticize them? We have the ability to shift and reframe the narrative we tell ourselves, giving us the courage to take action. Sometimes all we need is twenty seconds of courage to experience what we are capable of and to see what is possible.

Innovating, creating, truly being yourself, putting your unique ideas out into the world...all of these are vulnerable things that open the door for criticism and judgment. We can't expect to have an extraordinary life by making ordinary decisions, by going with the flow of society. But in the end, the ordinary, safe choice that never gets questioned or criticized by anyone ultimately hinders our ability to truly get to know our best. Having the mindset of being okay with what others may say or think aids in our ability to fully express what we have to offer to the world and to ourselves.

People are going to judge and criticize; the world can be a cruel place sometimes. I choose to view those individuals not as bad people but as ignorant and misaligned with me and what I value. What we do will not resonate with everyone, and that is OK. We are doing a disservice to ourselves and to others if we allow fear of judgment from others to win by not taking action and offering our uniqueness to those who seek it.

Here's an alternate way to say this: *YOU are under no obligation to be the same person others told you that you were five minutes ago.*

Attachment to "identity" is a form of resistance, a limitation that constrains the person we were meant to be. Too often, we accept labels assigned by others or by our own limiting beliefs.

We have the ability to change our path at any moment, without apology. As long as you are conscious of your decision and trust your intentions, you shouldn't feel guilty for accepting change as it comes.

Surround yourself with an environment that aligns with your values. Your story about yourself and what is possible for you will begin to change. That being said, you must continue to question everything so you don't fall victim to living in an echo chamber.

You cannot become a new person with the same personality. It is okay to change over time; in fact, it will be necessary to continue evolving into your best self. Doing so will look like this: changing your lifestyle, habits, routines, people you surround yourself with, your conversations, topics you discuss, your energy level, etc.

You can make a change in your life at any moment. We have the freedom to live the life we truly want to live, and we shouldn't feel guilty about making decisions that allow us to do just that.

YOU ARE THE DIRECTOR OF YOUR OWN LIFE. How you think and act on a daily basis determines the person you are destined to be. What's cool about this concept is you can change the narrative at any time. The key is to realize you hold the pen to rewrite the script.

One of the most common causes of failure is the habit of quitting when you are overtaken by temporary defeat. Almost everyone is guilty of making this mistake at one time or another. Before success comes in anyone's life, they are sure to meet with much temporary defeat and perhaps some failure. These setbacks are opportunities to build character and momentum. The more challenges we overcome, the more confidence we gain in our abilities. Proactively seek challenges so when the unexpected and unwanted events come your way, you will have the skills to handle any situation confidently with an inner knowing that all is good.

Daily action, done consistently, with a focused intent, and with an elevated emotion such as Gratitude...over time, the compound effect will begin to work in your favor. Show up consistently, and good things will happen for you!

Daily actions are completely within your control. Even if those actions are very small and don't feel like major progress toward your goal. Some examples of daily actions that have an impact on your future over time include who you surround yourself with, the conversations you have with others and with yourself (the latter is more important), the amount of effort you implement in your chosen field, and choosing the content you consume (social media, TV, news, books, podcasts, etc.).

Every person's day will look different; however, just know that whatever it is you're doing today has a significant impact on your future self. I'll say that again: just know that whatever it is you're doing today has a significant impact on your future self!

YOUR RESULTS ARE DETERMINED, IN PART, BY your actions. But a multitude of factors outside of your control, including timing, circumstances, and luck, all get a vote on how your best efforts turn out.

Remember, what gets measured gets managed. The elements you have the most control over are your effort and your intention. Have a way to measure your execution and maintain Gratitude for the process. Strive for excellent execution, not perfect outcomes. For example, if you're trying to write a book, a daily word count is a good goal. *The number of copies sold* is not.

Gratitude for the work itself will keep you going and sustain you through the ups and downs along the way. Through awareness and honest accountability, you can stay consistent and pivot when needed. Measure your execution, not the results.

The goal is to get better and better, not to pursue perfection. We can control our intentions and our actions; the results will come or they won't. Know that anything done with focused intent and focused effort is not a waste of time. Even if you don't get the result you're after right now, maintain Gratitude for the process, knowing that better opportunities are waiting for you.

Showing up consistently matters more than showing up perfectly.

We become our own unique version of the people we spend the most time with. Choose your inner circle wisely and remember that your best requires respect and honesty. We are all conditioned by our environment and by those we surround ourselves with. Put yourself in an environment that allows you to thrive. Our beliefs are often a reflection of the people we spend the most time with.

Think of those special individuals in your life who truly elevate you. The people who allow you to be the most unique version of "you" and bring out your best qualities. Those who encourage confidence in yourself with the belief that your personal best is yet to come.

I'm not referring to those people who simply tell you what you want to hear, not the yes people who agree with everything you say or do. Your ego loves those people. I'm referring to those special individuals in your life who truly hold you accountable to be your best. The people who allow you to be the most unique version of "you." Those who encourage confidence in you, instilling the belief that your best is yet to come.

A true friend is someone who knows all of your flaws and still chooses to love you anyway.

We are often much closer to achieving our goals than we think. We mistakenly underestimate what we can do in ten years, and we overestimate what we can do in one year. One good decision leads to more good decisions. For example, I believe the most important choice we can make starts from the moment we open our eyes in the morning. Choosing to focus our attention on Gratitude sets the tone for the day. This practice directs your focus onto the things and people you have in your life. You will start each day from a place of abundance rather than lack. This choice alone will lead to other great choices throughout your day.

You were born to be *real*, not perfect. No matter what you have done or haven't done, no matter what you've been through, one single choice can alter the direction of your day, your week, your year, and even your life.

"Comparison is the thief of joy."
Theodore Roosevelt

COMPARISON WITH MYSELF BRINGS IMPROVEment; comparison with others brings self-judgment and discontent.

Comparison isn't inherently bad. We must maintain an honest eye to evaluate where we currently are with the pursuit of where we want to go. This is how we level up. Sure, look to others for insights and inspiration, but don't fall into the trap of comparing yourself to others.

We humans tend to compare unfairly. As the saying goes, you can't compare your chapter one to someone else's chapter twenty.

Self-doubt from playing the comparison game prevents most dreams from ever getting off the ground. We torture ourselves with thoughts of what other people might think or might say. If we simply show up and do the work that inspires us and that we feel called to do, we would find a group of people who align with our craft and our style of expressing ourselves.

Simply expressing Gratitude can have lasting effects on the brain, which could contribute to improved mental health and our overall well-being. Try shifting your focus away from comparison and instead wishing Gratitude and blessings on others. When you can practice this consistently, there isn't much that can limit you from living your best life. Nothing anyone says, thinks, or does can have any effect on you anymore. What's interesting is that nothing changed but your mindset.

YOU STILL HAVE TIME.

The best time to plant a tree was twenty years ago. The second-best time is right now.

In *The Artist's Way*, Julia Cameron reminds readers that if you start "late" and worry about how old you'll be when you finally get good at whatever it is you're starting, you'll be the same age as you would be if you didn't try in the first place. So, start!

Rarely ever will you improve and look good at the same time.

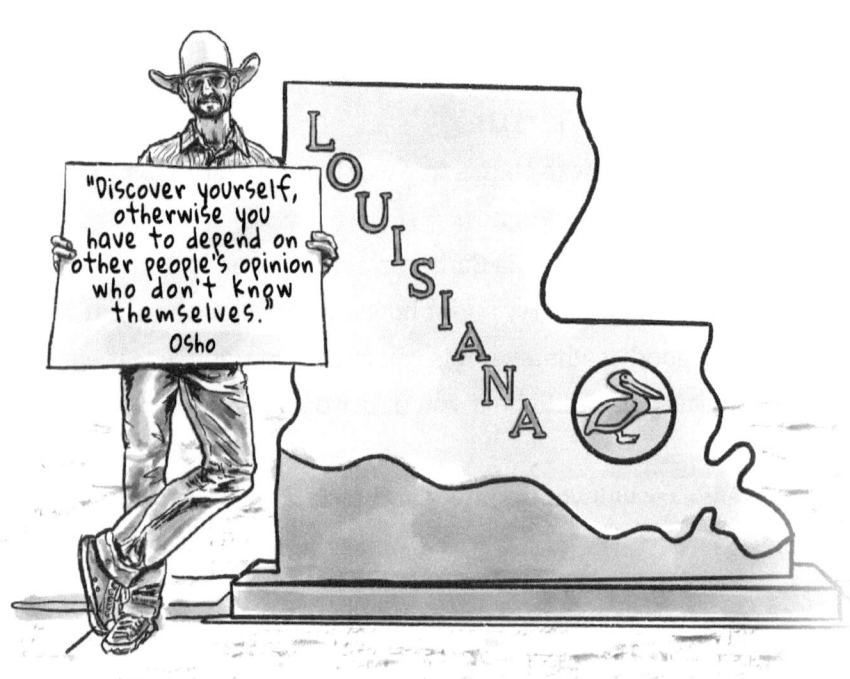

READ BOOKS, STUDY PHILOSOPHIES FROM THE greats, learn from others, and set forth on your path of self-discovery. The key is to internalize your lessons learned and make them your own. We are all conditioned by external stimuli; however, with awareness, we have the power to choose what we tune in to. Calibrating and recalibrating our antenna often allows us to stay in tune with a higher power.

We often find ourselves looking to others for the answers when they haven't even begun to look for themselves. If you wouldn't trade places with them, then don't seek their advice.

MEMENTO MORI IS LATIN FOR "REMEMBER YOU will die." This phrase sums up the ancient practice of reflection on our mortality. Socrates said *memento mori* is the proper practice of philosophy, which is "about nothing else but dying and being dead."

Remembering that we could leave this life right now may sound morbid and depressing to some. However, I encourage you to use this philosophy as a reminder to truly *live* every day.

Knowing we will one day leave this Earth should be one of the main motivators to experience all that we can while we're here.

Be humbled by death and be honored that you are lucky enough to experience Life.

Nobody gets out of this thing alive. Truly *live* and thrive; do not merely exist during your time here!

YOU ARE "YOU" AND YOU ARE ONE OF ONE. YOU are you in this moment, and in five minutes, you will be a different you.

Sure, you are allowed to want to level up and improve *yourself*. In fact, most ambitious people constantly desire a better version of themselves. This is fine; however, do not judge where you are in the process or journey of your life. Just because you want to level up does not mean you are failing at being the human you are today. This game of life is a process, and there is no destination, no finish line of achievement that you can cross until you take your last breath. The journey is the destination.

Recognize the opportunities for growth as they come and remain Grateful for the process. You can only be the *you* that you are at this moment with your current knowledge and awareness. Once you know better, do better.

There is a certain level of confidence that comes when you lean hard into your uniqueness. You are the only one who can truly know you.

SUCCESS IS ADMIRED, BUT THE JOURNEY IS OVERlooked. We live in a "microwave society" where we want instant results. We want fame, accomplishments, wealth, and nice things. We want them now and with minimal effort. We spend less time thinking about what it takes to get those things we want: delayed gratification, discipline, sacrifice, and sweat.

Think of someone you admire who is in the top 1 percent of the 1 percent of what they do. There are very few people in the 1 percent, even fewer within the 1 percent of the 1 percent. My point? The majority of the people you meet will not fall into this category, yet they can and will have an influence on the person you are and the decisions you make. When you look at the 1 percent today, their life probably seems great; they all have achieved something that others desire, be it money, fame, or wealth. The one thing others don't see? What they had to go through to get it. Sometimes we get a peek behind the curtain and hear of their rags-to-riches stories, but often they remain humble and keep their struggles to themselves.

It's easy to get caught up in the outside-looking-in game of envy.

People envy what the successful have, but few envy the sacrifices, struggles, and hard work it took to get there. Success is admired, but the journey is often overlooked.

Take a self-made entrepreneur, for example. People see the luxury car, the beautiful home, and the financial freedom, but they don't see the years of sleepless nights, the risks taken, the failures endured, and the moments of doubt that came before the success. They admire the outcome but wouldn't want to trade places for the grind it took to achieve it.

The same goes for athletes. Fans cheer for champions, but they don't envy the grueling early-morning workouts, the strict discipline, the sacrifices in personal life, or the pain endured along the way. They want the glory, not the grind.

ONCE YOU EXPAND YOUR *AWARENESS*, YOU CROSS a line of no return, and you never see the world in the same way. Most humans view the world through their own emotional subjectivity without ever realizing they are choosing a reality shaped by social conditioning and their own reactivity.

We all dance to our own tune, at least that's the intention. Not to be persuaded by societal expectations but, rather, move to your own beat. We will, of course, be misunderstood by most people. Realize there are few who will understand who you truly are. On the journey of personal growth, there are weird stages, "growth spurts," where you outgrow old circles of friends, and yet you don't quite fit into the next level yet.

The more aware I become, the more accepting and open-minded I am. At the same time, I've learned not to worry about the judgments from others and to be okay with whatever others may think or say and continue on with my own dance. To accept what is and to continue dancing to my own music is a beautiful thing.

Just because others might not be able to hear your music, don't let that stop you from doing "your dance." It's not about being better or worse than someone else; it's about being unapologetically who you are.

Freedom comes when we release all inhibitions and truly live every moment of every day.

THERE WILL BE MANY UPS AND DOWNS THROUGHout this game we call Life. This is inevitable, and most things we experience will be completely out of our control. However, what is in our control is the lens, our perception through which we view those ups and downs.

I think of the mantra I've been using for the past year or so: **"Everything that happens is the absolute best possible thing that can happen *for* you at that moment."**

This may seem like "fantasy land" for some of you, but this is the perception I *choose*; therefore, this is my reality. I'm not delusional. I am in control of my perceptions and therefore of my perspective.

However, I am human, and the default negative chatter and self-limiting beliefs are real; awareness is key. Having the awareness to recognize when I need to reframe or recalibrate my thinking is a constant practice.

What's for you won't go past you. Your path is your path. Tuning in to your awareness, you cannot miss what is for you. Gratitude must be the foundation for you to see your path accurately and clearly.

As we seek and search, our meaning and our purpose reveal our path, and our path reveals our meaning and purpose. Somewhat of a paradox. *You have to spend money to make money.* You have to spend Gratitude to find Gratitude. Self-discovery is an amazing gift.

THESE WORDS BY RUMI ARE THE FUNDAMENTAL element of the Law of Attraction. The universe will conspire to present you with what you seek. The magic is always in motion, whether or not we're consciously aware of it. It is important to remember that this "Law" works objectively, for good and bad, desired or undesired; therefore, it is wise to be hyperaware of what you think about.

The most important thing is to be aware of your attention and energy as it relates to the Law of Attraction and not become attached to an outcome or result. Instead, have a burning desire and show up with a focused intent along with Gratitude, as if the thing you want is already yours. Allow things to manifest in their own time and understand that everything that happens is happening *for* you and in alignment with the energy of your thoughts. Conscious energy will most often get us where we want to go much faster than an aimless approach.

We draw things closer to us with thought; our mind is much more powerful than we can even comprehend. Matter and our surroundings respond, far more than most people realize, to the power of thought. Remember, energy moves faster than matter.

Going one step further, we must not only imagine attaining our desires but also feel the emotions associated with that moment. Feel the Gratitude, feel the joy and excitement—as if you already have that thing. You are already doing this without realizing it, so why not be intentional with your thoughts and emotions, directing them toward the life experiences you want to have?

For you pessimists out there...the power of thought does not guarantee that what you think about will manifest 100 percent of the time, and rarely will it happen in the way you think or in the time frame you would like. However, our thoughts have a significant influence on the reality we experience.

Somewhat of a paradoxical relationship, isn't it? We have to be very clear and focused about the things we want to manifest: to combine a strong emotion with a desired intent and consciously keep them at the forefront of our mind through meditation, prayer, affirmations, reflection, etc., and at the same time let go and surrender to a desired outcome or result. Matter does not create consciousness; *consciousness* creates matter.

This concept has taken me years to even try to wrap my head around, and I'm not saying I have it all the way figured out. But I have experienced the power of releasing attachments and allowing the Law of Attraction the opportunity to work in my favor, which to me is the ultimate freedom in this game we call Life.

This is a constant practice of finding the balance between maintaining a focused intent and letting go of any attachments to any outcome or result. Every day is a practice, and that is all it is.

IF WE WOULD SIMPLY TAKE THE TIME TO GET CONscious and curious, realizing what it is that is causing the irritation we have with others, we could understand ourselves on a much deeper level.

It is impossible for another person to dictate or change our attitude; therefore, this feeling of irritation is essentially self-induced. The question is...how do we get out of our own way enough to view our perceptions objectively?

The goal is not to avoid becoming irritated. Rather, we can view it as an opportunity to expand our awareness, seek to understand where this feeling is coming from, and ask why we feel this way at this moment (without judgment toward ourselves).

So, when someone's behavior annoys you, it's time to get curious. Not about why they're acting that way but about why their actions bother you.

Using irritation as a tool and irritating people as teachers is an amazing practice to understand ourselves on a much deeper level. The intention is not to avoid negative emotions or to try to prevent them from arising. We're human, and they are going to come up. Feel all the feels—happy, sad, angry, irritated—and allow your awareness to grow.

I COME BACK TO THIS ONE WHEN I FEEL FEAR AND resistance start to creep in.

Often, the fear and resistance that prevent us from pursuing our desires and goals are made up of the stories and false narratives we make up in our own head. The negative self-talk and inner chatter play a big role in diminishing confidence in ourselves.

By far, the best way to overcome fear and resistance is to take action. We often fear the abstract, false narrative that we've created in our own mind about why we *can't* do a certain thing or why we *can't* achieve a certain goal. Overcoming each mental obstacle is an opportunity to build your mental muscles and expand your awareness. Awareness is key to noticing the unconscious, negative self-talk and then recalibrating our thinking to more positive thoughts that serve our highest self.

The ancestor of every action is a thought; so choose your thoughts wisely. A "reframe" that I've been leaning into lately is to think about best-case scenarios. When I feel the self-judgment or doubt set in, I use that feeling as a trigger to shift my mindset and ask, "What is the best-case scenario if I take action?"

By implementing this practice consistently, we trigger the possibilities and potentials to come our way, and doors begin to open that we could not even comprehend before. Ask yourself, *what if?*

My advice to myself...find the thing you love to do, and do that thing a lot. Over time, and with consistent focused action, the compound effect will take over, and the growth will be exponential. Then the cycle repeats itself. So find the next level of uncomfortable resistance and take the leap!

THINK ABOUT EVERY PERSON YOU LOOK UP TO or admire. What is it about them that intrigues you? What makes you pay attention to their work or what they put out in the world? Are they like everyone else, or do they show up in their own unique way, with bold confidence in their uniqueness?

The pressure to conform is constant, and sadly, most of us give in eventually. We think muting our originality and being uncontroversial is the way to avoid conflict and discomfort. And while that's true to an extent, conformity is also a sure way to avoid doing anything special and meaningful with your life.

To make a difference usually requires you to step out of your comfort zone of conformity and *be* different.

The goal is to become the best in the world at being you.

There's an interesting paradox at play here. You may worry that leaning into what makes you "weird" will isolate you. But what often happens is you set an example for others who are drawn in by your originality, just like you were by the role models who inspired you to be weird. Be you and watch how people align with that version of yourself. It's a pure and genuine feeling that promotes more confidence in your true self.

PERCEPTION IS ILLUSIVE.

Never reject an obstacle or boring moment because it doesn't align with your agenda. Whatever the present moment contains, accept it with Gratitude as if you had chosen it.

We do not heal the past by dwelling there; we heal the past by living in the present. Be Grateful for this moment, for this *moment* is your life. Remember, *your perception is your reality*.

Cultivate an attitude wherein you perceive every event or situation in your life, regardless of its nature, as the absolute best outcome for that specific moment. This perspective involves a deep trust in the unfolding of life, a radical acceptance of the present moment, and a conviction that every occurrence, whether perceived as "good" or "bad," is optimally aligned with your journey or larger purpose. This is not *naive optimism* nor *delusion*, but rather a clear mindset that focuses on what is within your control. This is how you recalibrate your perception.

Doing so can provide resilience, a sense of peace, and an ability to navigate challenges with grace, along with improving your overall well-being.

WE CAN OFTEN BENEFIT MORE FROM A SERIously bad day than we do from a slightly bad one. We tend to take action once the pain becomes intolerable.

There's an interesting phenomenon called the Region Beta Paradox: it theorizes that people can recover or make changes more quickly from more distressing experiences than from less distressing ones; that difficult events create better outcomes. It makes sense if you think about it: a mildly unpleasant experience might not inspire urgent action the same way a true rock bottom would. This paradox explains why many people who overcome serious trauma, addiction, and setbacks in life often go on to do great things and why folks who are moderately stuck and drifting through life often stay that way.

You don't have to hit rock bottom to make changes in your life, but it's good to know you can always reframe rock bottom as the ultimate catalyst for positive change. *There's nowhere to go but up.*

WHERE WE PLACE OUR ATTENTION IS WHERE we place our energy. This is the fundamental element behind the *Law of Attraction*.

The Law of Attraction is constantly at work, whether you're aware of it or not. So think about what you want in your life rather than the opposite, combining extremely clear and conscious thoughts with positive emotions and intentional action. Try to stay aware of the negative chatter when it arises and use it as a trigger to reframe your thoughts and your perspective. This is a continuous practice of reframing our thinking to "this is the best possible thing that can happen *for* me at this moment." *Nothing is good or bad, but thinking makes it so.*

On the flip side of this, I would be remiss if I didn't mention how important it is to feel all the feels. I don't want to paint a closed-off approach to life because I think it is important to feel the emotional pain too. We are humans, not robots. Allow yourself to grieve, feel the anger when it arises, and feel the sadness. Feel all of it without becoming overwhelmed and without suffering through the process.

When I am confronted with any obstacle, I return to the idea of *amor fati*. This mindset allows me to make the best out of anything that happens: treating each and every moment—no matter how challenging—as something to be embraced, not avoided. To not only be okay with it but to love it and be better for it. Like oxygen to a fire, obstacles and adversity become fuel for your potential.

Look for the Gratitude in any and every situation; it's easier to find that way.

"You can have everything you want in life if you will just help enough other people get what they want."
Zig Ziglar

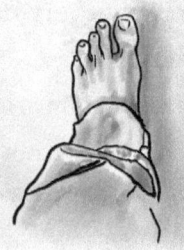
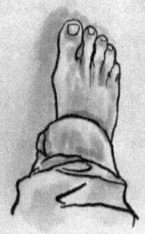

PROVIDE VALUE. REMAIN GRATEFUL FOR YOUR opportunity to provide value.

The Law of Reciprocity states that when you give value, money, or time, it will come back to you tenfold. Giving works much like a boomerang; however, when it returns, it will be bigger and better. If you're not getting what you want in life, use that as a sign to focus on what you're giving.

WHILE IT'S TRUE THAT YOU EXPERIENCE EACH of your thoughts, they don't always represent the truth.

Our senses can lie to us. Here's a simple experiment to prove this. Get a glass of water and a pencil. Fill the glass halfway with water. Drop the pencil into the glass and look at what appears to happen to the pencil when it is under the water. It gives the illusion that the pencil is much larger than it actually is. That's why we can't always trust what we see or think.

Awareness is key. Without it, we are subject to our past experiences and to the stories we unconsciously make up in our own head, most of which are simply untrue. Don't be afraid to call yourself out.

As our awareness expands, we can always look back on how naive we were a week ago, six weeks ago, a year ago, five years ago.

Negative self-talk stems from our beliefs and, at the same time, leads us to reaffirm our beliefs that we have of ourselves. This shapes our attitude, which ultimately leads to our perceptions of the world and how we live our lives and experience the world.

Realizing our true self-worth is simply a shift in our beliefs and our mindset. Most of the beliefs we have as adults were shaped by the social conditioning we experienced when we were young children. You begin to realize the choices are endless. Everyone is subject to social conditioning: "go to school, get a job, buy a house, live the American dream, and then you can be happy."

Becoming aware of the negative self-talk and beliefs is step one. Once we identify the beliefs that hold us back, we are then ready to find the path that leads us to becoming the highest version of ourselves. Knowing we become what we think about most and knowing we have the ability to control our thoughts makes me question why we ever allow ourselves to think anything but positive thoughts and why we would maintain any belief that prevents us from living our best life.

When the voice of negative self-chatter starts to creep into my head, I do my best not to judge myself for these thoughts, and then I get curious and ask, "Where are they coming from?" Most of the time, I can trace them back to "ego" or to an experience from my childhood. This genuine curiosity is beneficial to understanding myself and my mind on a deeper level, which provides the foundation for optimal growth and meaning.

We often ask the right questions to the wrong people.

Seek guidance from those who have been where you want to go in life. Do this by consistently surrounding yourself with people and mentors who are aligned with your journey and with the life experiences you want to have. Often, those people offering unsolicited advice don't know, and those who do don't offer until asked.

On a deeper level, it's about aligning with those who understand your vision. Whether you're navigating entrepreneurship, relationships, or self-discovery, the right guide—someone who's been where you're going—can make all the difference. This wisdom encourages intentionality, urging us to choose our advisors with care and focus on voices that truly resonate with our journey.

PEOPLE ARE GOING TO JUDGE, SO YOU MIGHT as well let them judge you for who you truly are. To allow them this opportunity, you must first seek to understand who you are for yourself.

You can't read the label from inside the jar.

When we fear criticism from others, we're often worried about what others may say or think about us, about what we're doing, and how we're doing it. **This is the ego talking**, and if we listen, it will prevent us from accomplishing the things we set out to do out of fear of judgment. We may think it's the opinions of others holding us back, but if the ego is involved, that voice of resistance is literally all in our head.

The most important thing to remember is that other people's opinions are out of our control. You have the freedom to choose whether you allow them to affect you in a negative or positive way. The truth is, most people want you to do well, just not better than them. Whether they consciously try to slow you down from envy or whether they unconsciously hinder your growth due to their ignorance, you must stay confident in your pursuit and know that what goes on in someone else's mind cannot harm you in any way.

I'd much rather be hated for who I truly am than be loved for who I'm not.

WHAT WOULD YOU DO DIFFERENTLY IF YOU knew nobody would judge you? They say to begin with the end in mind. What would you do differently today, knowing there will come a time when you look back on your actions? Would *future you* be proud of your actions?

This exercise isn't meant to be dark or morbid. Quite the opposite. By thinking about how your "life flashing before your eyes" is going to look, you remind yourself to celebrate life, focus on what's important, and make it count.

You owe it to all of us and yourself to get on with what you're good at while you're here.

WE MUST LEARN TO GET OUT OF OUR OWN way, to transcend our own thoughts and expand our awareness beyond our conscious minds, and to gain insights as to what's possible through the lens of Gratitude.

Umwelt is the technical term for the sliver of the data stream that we normally apprehend. It's the "reality" our senses can perceive. And all *umwelts* are not the same. For example, dogs hear whistles that humans cannot, sharks detect electromagnetic pulses, and bees see ultraviolet light while we remain oblivious. I believe the same is true for every human. Even though we have the same hardwiring, some humans are more aware than others based on their *umwelt*: their perceptions, their environment, and their conditioning.

Through awareness of *self*, you understand that you are not your name, and you are not your body. Awareness also plays a big role in seeing the opportunities and possibilities of the person you might become. This awareness is something that will continue to grow and build upon itself.

ONE CAN BE RICH IN POSSESSIONS BUT AT THE same time be poor in experience and meaning.

Money itself has no value. The value is what we are able to purchase with it; most people don't necessarily want millions of dollars; rather, they want to live a millionaire lifestyle.

The research on the psychology of money and happiness is surprising. According to a groundbreaking 2010 study by two Nobel Prize–winning economists, Daniel Kahneman and Angus Deaton, money actually makes you happier...up to a point. They found that self-reported happiness increases as income increases, but only up to $75,000 of income ($108,000 in today's money). After that, there is no correlation between money and happiness.

It makes sense when you think about it: If you are struggling financially or barely getting by, having more money is going to solve a lot of your problems, and you'll probably be happier. But you get to a point where *more* doesn't get you a higher quality of life or better experiences; it's just extra zeroes in your bank account. We get off track chasing money for its own sake, not realizing that some of the best things in life can't be bought.

My relationship with money is different today than it was just five years ago. My philosophy is that money comes in and money goes out. I firmly believe that having more money simply magnifies the person we already are today. If you are a person who does good things, having more money allows you to do more good in the world, and vice versa.

At some point, not too long ago, I realized I had an attachment to the idea of having a lot of money, stemming from social conditioning and a preconceived idea of what *success* looked like. I've realized it's not the actual money I was chasing; I was seeking to become the person that it takes to acquire millions of dollars.

Please don't misunderstand. I still want to make as much money as I possibly can and have zero guilt in saying that. However, I recognize that the money I make is simply a by-product of where I focus my attention and energy. What I value more than any financial gain is the focused effort and intention I put into getting it.

True wealth is found in relationships and experiences, not possessions.

YOGI BERRA PLAYED IN THE MLB FOR NINETEEN seasons, playing all but his last season with the New York Yankees.

Cultivating our mindset in a way that serves us and others is one of the most important practices we can focus on. Remember that it is a *practice* and one that requires consistent effort.

Start showing up consistently with a focused intent and in a state of Gratitude, taking one step at a time. Don't overthink it. With consistency and focused effort, the universe will recognize your intentions, and it will conspire with you. If your mind is filled with doubt and worry, the universe will recognize this and give you more to be worried about. And if you're Grateful and focused on your intentional and focused actions, the universe will give you more to be Grateful for and present more opportunities to you.

In baseball, there is a phrase that is said quite often: "*You need to have a short memory.*" It just takes one thought to change the trajectory of your life. Having a short memory doesn't mean forgetting the lessons you've learned from your mistakes; rather, it means not letting them stifle your growth. Focus on what you can control, and the only thing that falls into this category is your mind.

BUILD YOUR IDENTITY UPON THE ROCK OF CON-sciousness. Everything else is a castle made of sand on the beach at low tide. You are free to enjoy those sand castles; just don't get confused when the ocean of time sweeps them away.

Top regrets from people on their deathbed:

1. I wish I'd had the courage to live a life true to myself and not the life others expected of me.
2. I wish I had let myself be happier.

In reference to number one, we get caught in the social conditioning trap and aren't even aware of it most of the time. Thinking we have to have the cars, the big house, all the toys, and things to impress other people that often we don't even like.

Let me be clear, I'm not against making money or having nice things; however, I am very aware that they alone do not ensure happiness.

Living a life that others expect of you is never satisfying because, in doing so, you are always in search of external validation. Constantly in search of more, more, more, and there is never enough *more* to quench the thirst of external validation.

What gets me about number two isn't that they said they wish they were happier; rather, they wished they would've *let* themselves be happier. I feel like we've been led to believe life is supposed to be all work and no fun when we get to be a certain age.

Can you remember who you were before your "ego" showed up? Before your past experiences and attachments started to run your days? Before failure and judgment, or before an outcome or result dictated your mood?

How many people do you know who are merely going through the motions of life? They go to a nine-to-five job they hate simply for the money or because they think that's what they're "supposed" to do. They're doing what society deems "success," never realizing they are another victim of social conditioning.

Social conditioning is something that has been at work programming our brains since birth. No one is immune to social conditioning. This can be the result of TV, media, teachers, religion, or the actions of our parents and peers. The most common trap that most of us have fallen into at some point is conforming to the terms that society has defined as "success."

I was a victim of social conditioning at one time. I did the nine-to-five for a long time selling pharmaceuticals and was extremely "successful," according to society's standards, but I wasn't truly happy. I simply existed, doing what I thought I was "supposed" to be doing and letting the program run. Every day was the same. I was unconscious and unaware that I could be doing anything different. Though I felt the pull to do something else for years, I ignored the whispers. It wasn't until those whispers grew so painfully loud that I could no longer ignore them that I was forced to take action and make a change. Change cannot happen until the pain of doing what we're currently doing gets stronger than the comfort level that is holding us back.

I encourage you to seek your own answers. Realize you have a choice, and just because society may not agree with what is true to you, know that it's okay. To truly live and not merely exist, find the thing you love to do and do that thing a lot! Pursue your purpose.

IT ONLY TAKES ONE...

One thought, one performance, one moment. The trajectory of our life can change at once. One good decision leads to another. It's hard to make that decision with confidence if you are following others. *It's better to live your life imperfectly than it is to follow someone else's perfectly.*

Pursuit of your most authentic self holds the key to opportunities. In a single day, our life can take on new meaning.

There was a time in my life when I lived in fear and was constantly worried about what other people said or thought about me, or at least what *I thought* they thought about me.

I was completely wrapped in a blanket of narcissism and didn't even know it, which made life exhausting. Each day, I was striving to appear *perfect*, afraid to fail, and afraid to say or do something *stupid* in front of others. I lived every day in fear of being judged or thought less of by others.

I am now in a place where I am simply okay with what anyone may say or think about me. Sure, it still stings the ego a bit when I hear criticisms from others or get rejected by certain people or groups. However, with my awareness tuned to Gratitude, I am able to catch these thoughts before they spiral out of control and redirect them to a better perspective.

The thoughts you are aware of, you are in control of; the thoughts that you are not aware of are in control of you. As long as I know my intent is pure and true, then I can't let myself worry about someone else's perception of me. By living your truth and being okay with judgments from others, you will also begin to recognize the people aligning with that truth, and you'll notice other folks starting to fade away. Awareness is key to seeing it all more accurately.

The same is true for ourselves. No one outside of us can know what we really have going on inside our minds.

Overcome any judgement from others by following the words of Epictetus, "If anyone tells you a certain person speaks ill of you, do not make excuses about what is said of you. Instead, answer, 'He was ignorant of my other faults, else he would not have mentioned these alone.'" And keep moving.

The stories we create in our head are often far worse than what is actually happening in reality.

Sometimes we ask the right questions to the right people, but it's the wrong time. This means you're not ready.

I have always sought guidance from those who are doing more than I am and from those who are smarter than me. It does not always end in success. Forcing progress before one is truly ready can be futile.

When you are on a pursuit, giving everything you have, you will learn indirectly from others, and also, mentors and teachers will begin to show up unexpectedly. Sometimes the lessons come in very unusual ways and from unsuspecting people. In life, a "teacher" is not always a formal educator but can manifest as a mentor, a challenging experience, or even a moment of self-realization. You will then be ready to take your skillset to the next level with their guidance.

It must be a diligent and intentional pursuit. You must pursue your craft for the craft and for the process. It must be true. The teacher will recognize your efforts and provide guidance.

Meaningful guidance arrives precisely when an individual is open and prepared to receive it. This readiness stems from a state of curiosity, humility, and a genuine desire to grow, creating a fertile ground for wisdom to take root.

This aligns with the idea that personal transformation precedes external support; one must first seek knowledge or clarity within oneself.

By fostering a mindset of openness and diligence, the student creates the conditions for the teacher—whether a person, experience, or insight—to appear, guiding them toward deeper understanding and fulfillment.

I CAN REMEMBER WHEN I FIRST READ THIS. IT'S ONE of those simple quotes, yet it really made me stop and think.

Knowing that the most reliable way to predict my future is to create it, I found myself asking, "Why then do I still fall victim to 'getting stuck in a rut' or doing the same routines that I know aren't serving me in any way?"

We choose to think a certain way or not think a certain way. We choose to do something or not to do something. We choose to say something or not say something. We are always making choices, consciously and/or unconsciously. We are always one choice away from shifting the trajectory of our lives for the better.

THE FIRST STEP TO TRUE CHANGE IS TO CHANGE your self-identity. You've justified your habits with the story you tell yourself about yourself. As you change your habits, you will change your story about who you are.

What got you here won't get you there. I finally came to the realization that I can't become a better version of myself with the same personality. Change happens when we align with our truth, consciously letting go of all attachments and truly being okay with what others may think. This mindset requires consistent practice and attention, but it also gives us the ultimate level of freedom.

I am constantly asking to see beyond the vision that I can even comprehend with the limited senses I have. I'm constantly expanding my awareness to all possibilities.

As your awareness expands, you will gain insights and further your knowledge of what you believe to be right for you.

SOME OF THE BEST ADVICE IS SO SIMPLE.

PAIN IS INEVITABLE THROUGHOUT LIFE. WE EXperience physical pain and mental pain on many different levels. Falling off your bike as a kid isn't nearly as bad as a head-on collision. A breakup when you're in the second grade isn't nearly as bad as a divorce after twenty years of marriage with three children. None of these situations lasts forever, and none of them can be improved by wallowing in suffering long after the initial sting wears off.

Pain does not imply that you should suffer. Suffering is a self-induced choice. With conscious awareness, we have the ability to recognize an undesirable situation for what it is. We can choose to smile in the face of adversity. The skinned knee from the bike wreck and broken bones from a bigger accident will heal with time, as will the broken heart from both the childhood breakup and the divorce. The situations that involve pain present an opportunity for us to build character, and usually, the more pain we endure, the stronger our character becomes.

Choosing how you experience or perceive the unwanted will dictate your life experience. Most things we experience in life are out of our control. The one thing that can never be taken away from us is our freedom to choose our perspective.

PEOPLE HAVE CERTAIN BELIEFS BECAUSE THEY have been conditioned to believe them.

Are we choosing our path, or are we being led? I've come to believe the answer is both.

The better question is…are we conscious or unconscious in our conditioning?

Even in our most conscious state, we are still buying into our own beliefs. We are choosing something or someone to follow; that is our guide. We are conditioned, and our thoughts are manipulated by our environment and the people we surround ourselves with. This is happening all day, every day.

It is naive to think you are paving your own path without any outside influence. You may think you are doing it "your" way, and as unique as you may think you are, your "uniqueness" has been shaped by your conditioning.

We have the ability to choose how to condition ourselves and our minds. Just as people go to the gym, run, or swim to condition their bodies, we condition our minds through our experiences, our environment, and the people we choose to surround ourselves with. True freedom is the ability to choose these things. Are you consciously choosing how you condition your mind, or are you just going through the motions and letting society tell you what to value and how to think?

Failure is inevitable, no matter what you're doing. The only way not to fail is to not do anything.

We're often more afraid of the fear of judgment and criticism from others than the actual failure itself. Whether in business, sports, performing on stage, or running a race... everything we do has an outcome. We become worried and/or fearful of the outcome, and that creates anxiety about our performance, or, worse yet, it often hinders us from even beginning our journey.

Being scared to lose is a death sentence for any desirable outcome. Instead, prime your mind for the results you want to experience, and focus on ways to win. Feel the Gratitude for the event or outcome as if it has already happened. Train your mind and body to become very familiar with that feeling of success.

Fail early so you can succeed later.

A SEASONED DOOR-TO-DOOR SALESMAN WALKS up to a house after dozens of previous rejections, sweating from working all day in the summer heat. He rings the doorbell, and the lady who opens the door seems to be irritated from the start.

As he begins his presentation, she goes off on him, yelling and screaming. He had been warned about her by one of his colleagues who was waiting on the sidewalk. The salesman simply smiles at her as he backs away from the door and says, "Sorry for the inconvenience. Hope you have a blessed day."

The lady, now with a tear in her eye and somewhat baffled by the salesman's authenticity in his kind words, asks him to repeat what he said.

Now he's confused. "Which part?" he asked.

She said, "I just yelled and screamed at you, and you responded genuinely with 'Have a blessed day.'"

The conversation shifts and is now amicable. She invites him inside to continue his presentation.

As he walks into the living room, he notices a pistol on the kitchen counter and says, "You're not going to shoot me, are you?"

She looks him in the eye and says, "No, I just found out yesterday that my son died in a car accident, and just before you knocked on the door, I was about to blow my brains out."

Think for a minute if that salesman had reacted to her hostility with anger. We never truly know what someone else is going through, and we never know the potential impact we can have on others. She bought what he was selling, and they remain friends to this day.

Remember this as you go about your day: only when we are mindful and our awareness is tuned to the highest frequency of our best self can we recognize these moments and act accordingly. If we leave it up to our unconscious, we cannot assure the outcome; however, we are still responsible.

We are responsible for our part in contributing to the greater good. We must be honest and accountable with our actions and with ourselves. Not only will others benefit from our awareness, but our overall well-being will also reap the benefits.

OUR DECISIONS DICTATE OUR FUTURE. OUR thoughts dictate our decisions. Our awareness (or lack of awareness) dictates our thoughts. Expanding our awareness allows us to recognize our thoughts for what they are, which leads to more conscious and intentional decision-making.

The key is the consistent practice of expanding awareness around our own thoughts without judgment and to identify and notice if they align with our intentions and reframe when needed.

LET GO OF WHAT WE THINK OTHERS ARE THINKing. We often misinterpret our interactions with others. Nearly 75 percent of the communications that are received are interpreted incorrectly. Interestingly, many people consider themselves good communicators.

Focus on what is within your control. What is going on inside your own mind? Ultimately, that is the only thing within your control and the best way to interpret your *reality* accurately. Know your intentions, seek awareness, maintain Gratitude, and know that nothing anyone says or thinks about you has any power to do you harm.

NO ONE EVER GETS REMEMBERED FOR THE IDEA that only lived in their mind, the one that was never acted upon. And no one gets to benefit from that idea either. What's keeping you from taking action? Overcome the negative inner chatter that is holding you back or preventing you from pursuing your ambitions. Why not reframe the negative self-talk to a "best-case scenario" mindset? *What if...?* What if it does work out? What if it far exceeds my expectations?

What's possible is beyond our comprehension; when we combine a focused intent, consistent effort, a confident mindset, and deliberate use of our time, good things follow.

I often think...what if Michelangelo never pursued his craft as an artist because of fear of judgment or worries that he wasn't good enough? Same for Johnny Cash, Elon Musk, Steve Jobs, Michael Jordan...the list goes on. What if these humans hadn't diligently pursued their craft? What if they merely remained dilettantes or, worse, never started? There's a reason we remember their names!

And then I think about all the names I've never heard of because those people gave up, quit, or never even began. I wonder what they could've done, how many lives they would have positively impacted.

I encourage you to keep searching for the best version of yourself, keep showing up consistently, stay curious, and continue to level up. The universe is full of mystery and magic, waiting for our senses to grow sharper. It's okay to not know everything you think you need to know to get started. Simply begin. Wherever you are today and with whatever you have, start now, and your path will be revealed unto you.

As a person who likes to think a lot...I wasn't sure I believed this quote when I first read it. But after pondering on this, I have to agree.

I believe focused thought and preparation are important; however, I also believe the best way to overcome any form of resistance or fear is by taking action.

The secret to any form of success is to simply get started and remember, you don't have to be great to start, but you do have to start to be great. They say the best writing is in the rewrite...in order to rewrite, you must first write.

I would be remiss if I did not mention that anything worth doing is worth doing with intention. Therefore, it is vital that most of your actions start with a clear and intentional thought, a strategy or plan. The back and forth between focused thought, intention, and action is the secret sauce that everyone is looking for. If you are looking for the ultimate life hack, that is it. Combine focused thought with focused action while maintaining a state of Gratitude; you'll achieve more than you ever have, and you'll have meaning and purpose while you do it.

WE EACH HAVE A STORY WE TELL OURSELVES about ourselves. We do this consciously and unconsciously. Some questions to lean into: "Which story are we choosing to believe?" and "Who is directing this narrative?" Is it past experiences, other people, is it really you, or is it your ego?

Our *reality* is filtered through the lens of our perception. To put it simply: seeing is not believing; *believing is seeing*. We project our unconscious story into what we call "reality." We are often unaware we have the ability to prescribe the lens that changes our perception and perspective from negative and reactive to objective, proactive, and Grateful.

We never know what is going on in someone else's life or in their mind. No matter how great or how unglamorous that person's life may look from the outside looking in, we don't know their "reality."

So, if it is true that our life is shaped by our thoughts, why not consciously choose only the best possible thoughts? Only with clear and pure intentions will we be able to adopt the belief that everything happening is the absolute best possible thing that can happen in this moment. Choose your thoughts wisely...

REALITY DOES NOT DICTATE MY PERSPECTIVE; my perspective dictates my reality. To truly live an uncommon life, you must have uncommon views. View reality through your own unique lens and not someone else's distorted point of view.

How do you choose to see the world? Your choice is your *reality*.

Seeing the world through the lens of Gratitude—a lens that allows you to view situations in the most optimal manner—is a skill that gets better with focused repetition. Above all, Gratitude is a choice.

Without awareness, there seems to be a time delay in implementing Gratitude for any undesirable circumstance that you may find yourself in. The goal is to shorten the time it takes to become aware of your unconscious emotions. It's a fun game to play once your awareness is in tune with your conscious and unconscious thoughts.

THE BANNISTER EFFECT REFERS TO THE MENTAL shift that occurs when a significant barrier is broken, demonstrating to others that what was once thought to be unachievable is, in fact, possible.

This is a story about belief, clear vision, and a burning desire to achieve "the impossible." On May 6, 1954, Roger Bannister became the only person to run a mile in under four minutes, a feat that track athletes and experts at the time believed the human body could not handle. A physical and psychological challenge that many had pursued for decades before and failed.

Just forty-six days after Bannister did "the impossible," another runner broke the four-minute mile, and just a year later, three runners broke the four-minute mile once again in a single race. They now had the key, a confident belief that it was humanly possible.

Of course, there is a physical element to this race; not everyone is built for a four-minute mile. However, the most important lesson is to transform your sense of what is possible in your respective field. Find your gift and pursue it with everything you have and know that your mind is your greatest ally.

For a long time, I was in search of a "destination." Once I checked all the boxes and finally made it "there," I realized I was still searching for "more."

I had reached my monetary goals, I had a beautiful and successful wife, I owned a new house sitting on three hundred acres, I drove new vehicles…yet I still had a feeling of not being satisfied or fulfilled.

After going through a very dark time, I began the soul-searching journey that I am still on today. I learned that Gratitude was the integral piece I was missing. I was attached to the idea of "success," always wanting *more* without being Grateful for what I already had accomplished, which is a very tiring, never-ending cycle that almost always leads to insecurity, self-doubt, and burnout.

I realized I can be Grateful for where I am now, for the knowledge and "success" (however you define it) I have now, and still have the desire to be better tomorrow without feeling guilty. But the main ingredient is Gratitude.

Gratitude is not complacency.

One of the biggest lessons I learned was that *I'm not alone*, and neither are you. We're all just humans on a journey trying to figure out this thing called "life." Remember, no matter how perfect someone's Facebook or Instagram page looks, everyone has struggles and challenges every day. How we overcome these life hurdles is determined by our perception of them.

I try to remind myself of the following every day:

Have patience with the Journey you are on. The Journey itself is the destination.

Do your best not to judge yourself or others.

Trust that your intentions and your efforts are guiding you to exactly where you are meant to be.

You are learning the lessons you need to grow, and you are becoming the person you are meant to be.

It's all part of the process.

Stay Grateful for the process and allow the outcomes to come as they may.

Stay Grateful!

www.ingramcontent.com/pod-product-compliance
Lightning Source LLC
Chambersburg PA
CBHW060517080526
44586CB00012B/513